Believe

Prayers Are Miracle Possibilities

Michele Gayle

authorHOUSE®

AuthorHouse™
1663 Liberty Drive
Bloomington, IN 47403
www.authorhouse.com
Phone: 1 (800) 839-8640

Published by AuthorHouse 06/16/2017

ISBN: 978-1-5246-9233-9 (sc)
ISBN: 978-1-5246-9232-2 (e)

Library of Congress Control Number: 2017907928

Print information available on the last page.

This book is printed on acid-free paper.

Contents

Dedication

I dedicate this book to the loving memories of my mother, Reverend Dr. Cynthia L. Miller. The believers of "the way, the truth, and the life," and all spiritual truth seekers. May this book serve as a beacon, lighting the way, the path to your abundant life!

Introduction

Does prayer work? Asked Sam. "I've been praying for all my life, and I honestly cannot see anywhere in my thirty-six years where the Lord had answered one of my prayers I think it is only a matter of playing the hand you have, and that's all to it. God is not involved with our personal lives!" was his friend's swift reply. A frown like the falling of night on a summer's eve came over Sam's face, suddenly he appears so angry and retaliate as he said, "The Lord, what Lord? Certainly, he is against me!"

Maybe you have expressed similar sentiments as my dear friend Sam. Many of you too have lost faith in God's ability to answer your prayers. Rather ascribing to the belief that all God has done is to exact punishment upon you. You too maybe share the opinions of most people who believe that "God does care but not for you. He cares for humanity, but only in a general sense." Their thoughts are that "He is involved with us, but only as a people--- on a global basis---not individually."

That's a lie! Not at all true --- God cares about us and is involved in the smallest details in each of our lives as individuals. In the Bible, in Hebrews, He says, "Surely I will never leave you nor forsake you." Double positive, the New

Testament in Roman chapter eight says that nothing shall be able to separate us from the love of God!" John Chapter three and verse sixteen says, "God so loved the world that He gave His only begotten Son..." If God, therefore, has given Christ His Son as a ransom for all; how much more shall He by the same Christ also give us all things freely.

God affirms His love for humanity in Isaiah chapter forty- nine verse fifteen, He asked, "Can a mother forget her nursing child, that she should not have compassion on the son of her womb? Yes, they may forget," said He "but I shall not forget you." Does this sound like someone who does not care? Is this a person who only considers you occasionally? God does care for you. Acquaint now yourself with God and be at peace. That is a start to getting your prayers answered. Not some but all, not on occasion but all the time. Know God personally; He wants to reveal Himself to you. He desires good for you, not to do you harm; but to give you hope and future.

For I know the plans I have for you," declares the Lord, "plans to prosper you and not to harm you, plans to give you hope and future. Then you will call on me and come and pray to me, and I will listen to you. You will seek me and find me when you seek me with all your heart. I have myself been where you are now, and prayer was such frustration, boredom, and struggle. Fasting every week--- twice each week and, at the least a twenty- one or forty days of fasting per year. Most days praying morning and night, rising at three a.m. after having gone to bed at about 11:30 p.m. Or later; but all for naught it seemed. No answer in the areas of my life where it mattered. So, I understand the cycle---Praying every day, yet not seeing the desired results.

You've refused to celebrate the one or two answered prayers; because you see them as mere coincidences.

On the other hand, you as well had not taken notice of your answers when they came. There have been much more answers than you are aware. So then, where there should have been praise and thanksgiving; there was ingratitude. Why? You are not paying attention. Then you say God does not answer---all the time you have not taken the time to count your blessing. Hence your unfulfilled prayer life. Praying for an abundance of rain to receive a sprinkle. Prayer just isn't enjoyable, and at times you've chosen not to bother. Then, you are guilty because of your neglect of it. Returning full of zeal, to again lose interest, In turn, there is frustration--- not enough manifestations of answers vs. prayers to keep you excited about prayer. You need a renewed mind concerning God; who He is. Also, you need to understand what is prayer and how things truly are. I am going to in this book teach you how to get your answers every time you pray.

Your entire life is about to undergo an evolution---and A major shift and transformation in the way you think or perceive God. Your understanding of God is the key to your believing you have your answer to prayer. You can have the life you desire now If you truly believe in the way God has created all things. And all things are in alignment according to His loving plan and design for our lives. It is necessary to know that Heavenly Father is not merely involved in your life, but He takes special notice and participates in the minutest details. You should read Psalm 139 to hear for yourself. The Psalmist David knew that God was in all his life's details. He was involved in life before, and through his conception--- his life as a humble shepherd; to that of a mighty King; and equally so as a murderer needing forgiveness. The saint as well as the sinner, God loves you!

God is involved in the lives of ordinary people, as well as the infamous. He is so involved that He had planned and prearranged for every individual's personal good outcome even before our entrance into the womb. The entire universe is designed to come into agreement with you. It certainly is not a hostile world out there! So very often the lack of knowledge of the truth is the reason for our suffering. It is the God's truth you know that would set you free. "You shall know the truth, and the truth shall make you free" (John 8:3). You need to learn or relearn the amazing facts concerning manifesting your prayer; and how to get answers every time you pray. Change the way you view prayer, and ultimately eradicate the routinized prayer from your life. The flames of prayer will ignite, immediately you will begin to see a radical transformation in your life; As Dreams and desires manifest as you desire them. You can have every answer to your prayers and without delay! It is up to you, however, to "believe" and to tap into this new life in the Spirit; A life without lack. One of love, joy, and peace. You will exceed limitations, thoughts, and imagination; A life where daily miracles are your typical.

It is the truth! You and everyone else can have the answer to every prayer, every time you pray. It is already so for me and countless many. Why not you? Jesus said, "for verily I say unto you, that whosoever shall say unto this mountain, be thou removed, and be thou cast into the sea; and shall not doubt in his heart, but shall believe that those things which he saith shall come to pass; ye shall have whatsoever ye saith" (Mark 11:23.) These are the truths that I have been practicing for almost ten years now. And have for the past six years seriously committed myself to so living. I live with certain expectations. These expectations are never altered, or compromised for any reason. I rather not talk about those things that are not favorable to me. I do not frequently speak to certain people. Especially those too clueless, and tough headed to change their thinking. Regardless of what is present, I expect what I desire, and they bloom in their season---at the point of need. You are in control, and the creator of your world, by your attitude; belief, thoughts, and feeling.

You say or recite very familiar Scriptures and more without results. Why? Lack of understanding! There are natural and spiritual laws at work, and there must be the knowledge for correct application. The teaching of Christ have both spiritual and natural application; belief in God's truth as they apply to us are of vital importance. Faith comes by hearing and hearing by the word of God. You cannot possess what you do not believe. In Mark chapter nine verse twenty-three Jesus said; "Everything is possible to them that believe." That says that those who do not "believe" will not enjoy the fruits of endless possibilities. My desire is to reveal these truths to you. They are transforming my life daily, and I want you to join me on this path.

The way is knowing that all things are in harmony with you when you are harmonizing with God the Creator and Infinite Source. If you will "Believe" "every prayer is a potential miracle!" Miracles will become your normal! You will frequently manifest what others will call unbelievable. People for loss for words---at their amazement will declare

Therefore, I tell you, whatever you ask *for in prayer,* believe *that* you *have* received it, and it will be yours. ~ Jesus the Christ

Chapter One

Believe God's revelation of Himself

Believe, is a conviction of something as being true. Believing is power, and when belief is love base, it is dynamic. Faith in the heart will always produce the extraordinary. God is perfect love. Love is the greatest and most powerful emotion! You tap into the great infinite power when you experience and know the character of God---that He loves you, and you are in awe of Him. There, is the beginning of a life full of miracles.

God is love, and He loves us, His desire and plan are for our good. It is the truth without fail, without partiality. He desires for you to have good things. As a matter of fact, more than abundant. God will reveal Himself to you in the next few lines of this chapter, please think on and "believe" His revelation, and let Him transform your life. Even as many believers, and I, and countless others of scriptures had personally encountered Him; desire, and expect your personal encounter. As I have said, the Divine always seeks to reveal Himself to us. Regardless of our faith, or religion---He aims to draw us to Himself. Even those who do not now believe. Seek, and you shall find--- knock, and the door will open unto you.

In the Book of Exodus chapter three, Moses was out tending his flock of sheep. The atmosphere about him for days seemed different. But he could not put his finger on it. More and more those days he had been thinking about back home in Egypt to the point of home-sick. Overwhelmed and steeped in melancholy he smells the scent of smoke; and the crackling sound of fire. Turning to see what was burning quickly he realized that he was encountering something extraordinary. Upon this knowing he moved closer towards the phenomenon; and, to his amazement, he heard his name called and the voice like smoke rising from the midst of the fire. "Moses, said He, "remove your sandals from your feet, for the place you are standing is holy!"

Moses understanding, he was having an encounter with the Divine in the burning bush; he prostrated himself--- the posture of worship! Exodus chapter three and verse seven to eight records, "The Lord said, "I have indeed seen the misery of my people in Egypt. I have heard them crying out because of their slave drivers, and I am concerned about their suffering. So, I have come down to rescue them from the hand of the Egyptians and to bring them out..." God will never fail; He will never disappoint---our cries He will never ignore, they do not fall on deaf ears; He always comes on our behalf! When we call, He shall answer and that right early. His loving-kindness is better than life.

The discourse continued thence between God and Moses, and The Holy One commissions him back to Egypt. Henceforth Moses' mission to free the Israelite people who are in slavery there. Considering that Moses was wanted for murder in Egypt; he needed some security. It was critical to him to have adequate preparations. That he has guaranteed protection, good back-up, qualified and substantiated information. So, he asked God "when I go to the people, and they ask me," "who sent you?" "Whom should I say have sent me?" God answered Moses thus: "Tell them, "I AM THAT I AM" have sent you!" Moses did as he was commissioned. He returned to Egypt, carrying the anointing in his hand, the presence of God before and behind; and the name of God "I AM THAT I AM" in his mouth and heart. In all of Moses' encounters, he was victorious and successful against Pharaoh and all unfavorable conditions, because he had the power of "I AM" with him and Israel. At every turn, I AM's presence made Moses as a god before the Pharaoh, and the people.

There is in I AM THAT I AM that assurance which changes our hearts and transforms that which is unfavorable to our desires. God the "I AM" is ever present in everywhere and in all things. I AM THAT I AM, is Eternally self-existent; Alpha and Omega, the Creator of all, sustaining of all; and abiding forever in all.

The original Hebrew which Moses spoke would have rendered the title "I AM THAT I AM" as EHYEH ASHER EHYEH. These words in themselves are intensely powerful. They are high vibrations of creative or miracle energy. This name that Moses was given to use is said to have been a code. As one who meditates, I know the power of the "A," "EH," "AH," and "HA" sounds; it is the sound which emanates the energy of miracles. This name of God was the power source for Moses' many miracles. The Hebrew people have from about the 2nd. Century B.C held the name of God in highest reverence. They refuse to speak the name of God and had chosen rather to use the Tetragrammaton YHVH (Yod, He, Vav and He) upon the utilization of any of these names you are mobilizing Omnipotence. There is power in and through the name of Ehyeh, Ashar, Ehyeh; the Supreme self-existing One.

Meditate on this truth as He reveals Himself to you. Believe and accept that He is as He had revealed. You can walk on water, or go through it on dry land---Any which way you get across to the other side of the flood is a miracle. It is a matter of perspective. You can manifest an ocean of fresh water in desert place; You can move mountains. Every prayer is a miracle! The Supreme Being, our heavenly Father, is always seeking and creating opportunities to make Himself known to us. Forever He desires intimacy with His humanity.

Moses encountered I AM in a burning bush, a cloud and a pillar of fire. In the city, as well as in the desert and on the mountain's heights. No place is too small, too low, too wide, too high or too dark that His presence will not reach. He Is kind and compassionate to you; indeed, the Divine will in all love and grace comes down to you. For surely as He had revealed Himself to Moses and Israel saying, "Tell them, I AM THAT I AM have sent you!" Whereby revealing an infinitely reliable and ever available present source. I Am That I Am, stands now attentive and alert to your call. You are more than a conqueror!

I repeat that God is forever seeking and creating opportunities to reveal Himself to us. It is for us to open to Him. I believe that Christ stands aloft to behold our hardheartedness; as He had wept over Jerusalem. Even so, today He weeps for us.

If only, He can so gather us unto Him as the hen gathers her chicks under her. May we look for Him--- for surely, He seeks for us---intimately He desires you and me.

About four years ago I had a supernatural experience. It was during the winter, and I had gone to the Virgin Islands to get away from the cold Canadian winter. Without fail each day I'd watched the sunset--- I love sunsets. Moonlight is no different; I love gazing out into the moonlight skies. One night my best friend took me up on a hill. A beautiful hillside, looking out into the Atlantic Ocean. It was most tranquil, the only sounds I heard was that of the breaking waves of the ocean against the rocks, the beautiful chirping; and whistles of the creatures of the night. The moon was beautiful--- a full moon. I walked a few feet away from my friend as though to walk away towards a full moon. Straight away I began to worship God as though speaking to the moon. Acknowledging the splendor of his majestic creation; His wisdom so exceedingly past finding out!

As I stood there in absolute awe of God, He spoke to me; (as though from down inside me and by a very deep impression.) He said, "I am not merely the God of creation you know!" And just as I was about to think, "I know that." He said "look!" and with that command to "look," I was transported into space. By a snap of the finger actually---Instantly as He said: "look!" I was in this other place. Instantaneous too I became aware that space is not space; rather it is like a television that is on but not receiving signal. A sort of static, pulsating, energy. However, He seemed to have implied that this is who He is. As the voice told me to "look" this massive wall of space stood before me; encompassing me, and yet I was in the space.

Space was not emptiness as we think of space, but it is full of force. It is very powerful, standing still--- as though observing me; yet it is not stationary! It is pulsating, electricity, a pulsing wavelike dark grayish--- an almost blackness. It virtually appeared stable, yet not; but more so I'll say it had a great depth to it. As well as tremendous energies. I also saw flashes of lights like little crisscrossing and overlapping strings running through it. It had unyielding pulses like heartbeats or brain waves. There was quietness yet I heard a sound or sounds much like a very high frequency. I felt it as well---this sound was also in my heart. This same vibration I have felt its in my heart, body, also I have been hearing it in my ears for quite a while now; for few years before this encounter. The same energy outside of me is me---I am of the same high power, I am, you are also that same energy, and all things are of that intense energy. In Him, we live and move and have our beings.

We are of our Father God; of His image and likeness! Initially, I had kept this revelation to myself. Choosing only to tell a couple of persons about my encounter. Now I want to tell everyone---now that I know what it means. God is not anything at all as we have perceived Him to be. He is if I dear say: great intelligence and exceeding vast energy; beyond what words can express. I see and feel Him in the spaces about me---yes, I feel the presence of "I AM" in all of what is considered space or emptiness.

"I AM" fills all---therefore making it so easy for me to touch Him--- or rather I affirm that indeed He touches me. He touches you, all about you is I AM's presence. And it overwhelms me to tears, a bit of gladness really--- Just an emotion that at this moment I should praise, say something;

but I restrain myself and instead permit my fingers to move---dancing to the melody; a harmony of a heart and mind made one with the Divine. The candle on the stand seems to know it too. Like tongues of fire Its reflection casting on the wall most rhythmically, swaying to my music a praise glorious---I tell you now and again there is no "nothing," His formidable presence is filling all things, and reaching all people.

"Behold I stand at the door and knock," says He," "if anyone hears my voice and will open the door I will come in." In Him, I live and move and have my being! Just recently as I was looking at an online program via YouTube, I saw a video program bearing the picture of a gentleman I thought I had met in an airport weeks prior. A picture of Sir Garfield Sobers hanging over our heads provoked a conversation regarding his knowledge of cricket, as we waited in the customs and immigration line. Out of curiosity, I decided to view the video, which I Initially thought to have been about the power of the subconscious mind. I had some years ago studied it and adopted some of its principles. The truth is, I thought and knew there was more; but what I could not explain. It was very frustrating not being able to talk to others about it. Honestly, up until now, I thought most humbly that I was the only person with this revelation. I honestly feared that I was the only one given this revelation knowledge, however, what was revealed to me was also revealed to scientists.

Inquisitively I began to watch the video--- the speaker was the man I thought to have met at the airport. A scientist named Gregg Braden. I listened to Mr. Gregg Braden and literally, in a couple of minutes into his lecture he said these words: "There is an experience that we can have in our bodies that sciences had not allowed for until now." He continued to say, "Two assumptions of modern science are that: One, space is not empty--- it is full of a living essence, a living material. Two that we may have experiences in our bodies that influence our world beyond our bodies; through the conduit of what is in this space." Exactly the understanding and wisdom I needed ---this was God's revelation to me up on that hill on that beautiful moonlight night. And this man a scientist is confirming for me what I had seen. As well what I believed though not having a full understanding of it.

Now I know that what was shown to me, is in fact, the mind of God. Conscious Intelligent Mind, that modern day scientists call: "The Field"; "The mind of God" and "The Matrix." Today I am studying and practicing "the mind of God," and it is manifesting in my life. My perception of who God is transforming, due to my experience on the hill top! Because of the revelation of God, I no longer see persons as I once did; the conditions, prejudices are done. Now, I love without judgment and discrimination, well I try my hardest best to do so; the old mind always seems to get in the way. Now I understand much better our significant human complete dependence on the Divine Source.

Hitherto, we cannot live without knowing, and experiencing God. This awareness of the mind of God has eradicated the fear of what may, and what if from my heart, because I know the power and "presence" of God, in all. What ifs do not matter. I do not fight or struggle to control my life. No need, all things are as they should be; Divine intelligence is in control. Being in alignment with the Omniscient, my life is in complete surrender to Him;

and His way in all things. I find the way of Christ and His Divine truths to be much clearer. I tell you the truth; all things are possible to them that believe.

Being followers of Christ, it is quite necessary for me to present the truth of who God is as revealed by Jesus. Our great Teacher appears to be the first Prophet of the Bible to introduce God the Divine source as our Heavenly Father. The reference to God as Heavenly Father is prevalent throughout his ministry life. He constantly referred to God as Father. Most strikingly is the presentation of the Divine I AM THAT I AM as our "Heavenly Father." It is, therefore, essential for us to look at the first times that Jesus had referred to God as our Heavenly Father.

In Matthew chapter five and verse forty-eight he said, "be perfect, therefore, as your heavenly Father is perfect." Also in the Gospel of Matthew sixth chapter and verse fourteen, it records thus: "For if you forgive other people when they sin against you, your heavenly Father will also forgive you." A very key verse, which speaks directly to God and His attitude towards our good is Matthew chapter six and verse twenty-six. "Look at the birds of the air; they neither sow [seed] nor reap [the harvest] nor gather [the crops] into barns, and yet your Heavenly Father keeps feeding them. Are you not worth much more than they?" Jesus presents heavenly Father's involvement in human's lives on every level. From the Spiritual, Emotional and the Physical or natural.

On the *Spiritual*: he said, "be like heavenly Father" speaking to our spiritual maturity. *Emotional:* as regarding social issues, He said if you forgive others when they sin against you, God will justly and willingly forgive you your sin. *Physically*: he addresses our welfare and well being making it crystal clear to us that God cares and is thoroughly involved with all His creation. He is involved with us as a Father--- only however as the holy righteous Father, who is more than well able, and willing. All things are according as He had designed for us to thrive and be in wholeness. There is also Jesus' example of prayer to the disciples---what we refer to as the "Lord's or our Father's Prayer."

According to the gospel's account of Matthew Jesus taught thus: "After this manner, therefore, pray ye:" Our Father which art in heaven hallowed be thy name. Thy Kingdom come, thy will be done on earth as it is in heaven. Give us this day our daily bread and forgive us our debts as we forgive our debtors. And lead us not into temptations, but deliver us from evil: For thine is the kingdom and the power, and the glory, forever. Amen."

Was it the intention of the Rabbi for his disciples to recite this model prayer. Or was it his intent that his followers' attention may turn from the outwardly projecting egoistic self to the inwardly reflective true self---which is broken and contrite. Could it be that his intentions were to direct our attention and complete dependence upon Heavenly Father--our Divine and infinite source? One thing I am certain of is that He intended to raise the disciples understanding and knowledge of prayer. Their thinking and attitude about prayer and manifesting their desires had to undergo a transformation. Hence their request "teach us to pray." In other words, they wanted to know how to demonstrate what they desired. They wanted to show the power as did their teacher---the Christ.

The prayer is directed thus: One to Heavenly Father.

Two Heavenly Father's proximity is as far as within oneself. As by the Teacher's words, "heaven is within you;" also "the kingdom of God is within you." He is not far, far off! Third, Heavenly Father is holy, and thus we must give Him reverence; "hallowed be thy name." Fourth, one should recognize His kingdom at work in all things and consent to its Supreme governing authority. As His constitutions continue forever sure in all realms, so I acquiesce to its governance over me. All its powers, rights, privileges, and control. We must be acutely aware of these truths, holding them dearly in our hearts. The Lords prayer is an attitude more than a chant or recitation to be said. It evokes an attitude of surrender, having this attitude one is forever in prayer; always praying, without ceasing.

According to Jesus, God "I AM" is our Heavenly Father. He is holy and desires us to be like Him. He forgives us our sins, even as we forgive others their sins against us. All things are of Father and thus He provides and sustains all--- both small and great. Justly, the sparrow can look to Him and receives his essential supply. As well the lion He prepares its prey. To humanity, Heavenly Father opens His hands, and they are full of good things. It is one thing for any person to assume to speak of another; but who knows me as I do myself? I know me more than anyone else possibly can. As a matter of fact, your perception of me could be so very wrong. I have told you of God's revelation to me. Now let us allow the Sovereign Holy and Self- Existent One to give us a revelation of Himself.

We will for that reason look specifically at the book of Job chapter thirty-eight. As we consciously search for Him, He will reveal Himself. Job in all his calamity flanked about by friends who had no keen understanding of the nature of God. So critically they opened their mouths in matters too high for them. Provoking Job to lows unimaginable; even that of proving his self-righteousness before the Holy One. As well, he was trying to show the unfairness of God's treatment of him. Could you imagine that the Most Holy should defend Himself against Job's accusations? He, however, does so most graciously and without offense. I believe that Job had attracted this experience into his life. He was very sin conscious that he offered sacrifices just in the likelihood that his children may have sinned. Indeed, the thing that he feared most came upon him. Why? Because whatever we think of continually will manifest in our life.

Every time God will deal with humankind it is from the perspective of His great love; grace and mercy. Oh, what condescension--- the Eternal reaches down to his man, and in such grace, the sovereign raises him up again. Thus, He speaks to Job from the whirlwind:

"Who is this that darkens counsel by words without knowledge? Gird up now your loins like a man, and I will demand of you, and you declare to Me. Where were you when I laid the foundation of the earth? Declare to Me, if you have and know understanding. Who determined the measures of the earth, if you know? Or who stretched the measuring line upon it? Upon what were the foundations of it fastened, or who laid its cornerstone, When the morning stars sang together and all the sons of God shouted for joy? Or who shut up the sea with doors when it broke forth and issued out of the womb? —When I made the clouds the garment of it, and thick darkness a swaddling band for it, and marked for it My appointed boundary and set bars and doors, And said, Thus far shall you come and no farther; and here shall your proud waves be stayed? Have you commanded the morning since your days began and caused the dawn to know its place, so that [light] may get hold of the corners of the earth and shake the wickedness [of night] out of it? It is changed like clay into which a seal is pressed; and things stand out like a many-colored garment.

From the wicked, their light is withheld, and their uplifted arm is broken. Have you explored the springs of the sea? Or have you walked in the recesses of the deep? Have the gates of death been revealed to you? Or have you seen the doors of deep darkness? Have you comprehended the breadth of the earth? Tell Me, if you know it all. Where is the way where light dwells? And as for darkness, where is its abode, that you may conduct it to its home, and may know the paths to its house?

You must know, since you were born then! Or because you are so extremely old! Have you entered the treasuries of the snow, or have you seen the treasuries of the hail, Which I have reserved for the time of trouble, for the day of battle and war? By what way is the light distributed, or the east wind spread over the earth? Who has prepared a channel for the torrents of rain, or a path for the thunderbolt, to cause it to rain on the uninhabited land [and] in the desert where no man lives, to satisfy the waste and desolate ground and to cause the tender grass to spring forth?

Has the rain a father? Or who has begotten the drops of dew? Out of whose womb came the ice? And the hoary frost of heaven, who has given it birth? The waters are congealed like stone, and the face the deep is frozen. Can you bind the chains of [the cluster of stars called] the Pleiades, or loose the cords of [the constellation] Orion? Can you lead forth the signs of the zodiac in their season? Or can you guide [the stars of] the Bear with her young? Do you know the ordinances of the heavens? Can you establish their rule upon the earth?

Can you lift your voice to the clouds, so that an abundance of waters may cover you? Can you send lightning, that they may go and say to you, here we are? Who has put wisdom in the inward parts [or in the dark clouds]? Or who has given understanding to the mind [or to the meteor]? Who can number the clouds by wisdom? Or who can pour out the [water] bottles of the heavens? When [heat has caused] the dust to run into a mass and the clods to cleave fast together? Can you [Job] hunt the prey for the lion? Or satisfy the appetite of the young lions When they couch in their dens or lie in wait in their hiding place? Who provides for the raven its prey when its young ones cry to God and wander about for lack of food?"

Utilizing these rhetorical questions, God vividly reveals Himself: The Alpha and Omega, Ancient of Days. Creator, Guardian, and Provider. All-wise, and All-powerful. All seeing, all knowing and ever present! The God of all creation, heaven and earth, and all that there is and ever will be--- had He ordained. He had spoken, and who can dis-annulled. His wisdom beyond understanding; who might render Him counsel, or He might dear reprove? God is Omniscient, Omnipotent and Omnipresent. God, the creator of all things. He is Love. Not simply by what He does, but rather who He is--- unconditional and pure Love. Despite who we are, still, has He chosen us in love. It is not by works that anyone should boast, it is the gift of God.

Salvation is at work in all things---all that is needful for life and godliness He had provided and so very great is His faithfulness. "Believe" I AM THAT I AM - and experience the more than abundant life---life in the supernatural.

"I am the Alpha and the Omega," says the Lord God, *"who is and who was and who is to come, the Almighty"* (Rev. 1:8.)

Chapter Two

Believe your prayers are miracle possibilities

God is love! His love for us is everlasting; perfect, without limit, or end. It is by His perfect, and sincere affection for us that He had designed all things. Therefore, everything is organized to give way; to accommodate you and me in the earth. Jesus taught in the gospels saying, if you have faith as a mustard seed and would say to this mountain be thou removed into the sea, it shall be as you say. Also in his teaching on prayer in Matthew chapter six verses five and six. He instructs, "when you pray, enter into your closet." What is the closet but, your secret place of the heart or mind? You do not have to depart to any faraway places, nor climb to some high mountains. Although sometimes it is necessary to withdraw from society and the hustle and bustle.

There is always full access to your heart. In all conditions without fail at any time of day or night---all you need do is shut the door, in the quiet and private place of your heart. It is there in silent prayer and meditations--- that prayer is effective. There, in the secret of our hearts is where thoughts and emotions are united, thus producing the evidence of the thing desired. God who sees in private shall reward you openly. "Whatsoever you believe in your heart when you pray, believe that you have it, and it shall be so."

"Believe," or "Belief" is the operative word. Understand therefore that "whatsoever" you think that you will have. The feeling that you catch a cold every time you get wet; will attract that to you. Do not believe and think on the thing you do not want. It is for you to know--- that all things are possible; because God has created all things with endless potentiality. All things are possible if you will "believe." Belief is conviction---conviction fuels passion, and passion will always move you. Passion ignites in the heart will display a corresponding emotion all around you. This power changes the unfavorable conditions; aligning them to your belief and expectation.

Therefore, you have what you pray--- this is how you pray effectively. Knowing is the confidence, the assurance or guarantee; you will get your answer to prayer every time. Thus, your prayer must first move you before it can move the mountain. Hence the saying of James chapter two and verse fourteen, "faith without works is dead." One that is truly convicted will move mountains by their commands! Jesus says, "if you shall believe nothing shall be impossible for those who believe." All living things are created subject to human---the human has that authority and dominion. God has given us the powers within to have the rule over all things. Things --- matter is subject to you. Therefore, you can affect your world by your beliefs, thoughts, and words. That is just the way it is---I wish you will apprehend that. It is the way things are---everything is subject to your current belief in your heart---your belief changes them. Your circumstances are arrested and brought into alignment with your beliefs.

Believe in your heart---means to surround yourself with the feeling or emotion of "I have what I desire now." Love, Joy, gratitude and peace are the feelings of the heart. These flow from a place of love. If your heart is thus full of love, joy, and peace. Your desire--- who can therefore deny? Be happy, be motivated to "be" ---you can achieve anything! Mark chapter eleven gives a view of a condition of which Jesus and his disciples were facing. Jesus was hungry and seeing a fig tree he had certain expectation---to find something for them to eat. Never the less to his disappointment there was no fruit on the tree--- only green leaves. Jesus then cursed the fig tree.

There was nothing present for him to work with; he could have caused a miracle of increase if only there were one fruit on the tree. But he could not desire a miraculous appearance of figs. For him to do so would have been a violation of natural laws. We must always respect natural laws, and not disrupt them. He may have cursed it because of its barrenness. Magic does exist, and you can have a lot of things, by that power. However, to undermine the natural flow of things is punishable; there is always the karmic effect! People will say, things like God is punishing me when it is merely the consequences of their choosing---natural consequences.

The scripture says that immediately the fig tree withered up. Instantaneously Jesus had what he said. However, on the next day they returned; and Peter was amazed that the tree had tried up. Jesus in response to the disciple's amazement told them to "Have the faith of God." "If anyone shall say to this mountain, be thou removed and be cast into the sea, and shall not doubt in his heart. But shall believe it will happen, it shall be so for them." What is the faith of God? Belief in the heart; which changes the unfavorable condition of a thing---manifesting the specifically desired reality. It is a now faith, "Faith is said to be the substance of things hoped for, and the evidence of things not seen (Heb. 11:1.) In other words, it is the guarantee, the Title Deed. Faith is always present and active "now!" You have what you pray "now"! Consequently, we do not think we have the answers now and as such react accordingly; as though not having the thing now. For that reason, many are frustrated with prayer. Praying and not seeing the results.

You can have your prayer answered every time. The key contained in the text is that "belief," as well as desire, must be united in the heart. Whatsoever you desire in your heart when you pray believe that you have it, and it shall be so for you. That tells me a couple of important facts: One-Belief is critical to answered prayers. Two-Pray the thing desired, be specific. Three-The desire must be rooted in the heart. It is important because the heart is the seat of our emotions. In the heart, we believe. Also, it is in the heart that we feel or have emotions. Our emotions are either of Love or Fear. If thoughts and emotion are Love base, it fosters love, joy, peace, contentment, gratitude, thankfulness and compassion.

These produce the corresponding response---gratitude, joy, peace, and happiness. These improve our health and life all round. Manifesting our thoughts and desires. If thoughts are fear base, it produces doubt---feelings of frustration, anger, bitterness, greed, etc. These lead to lack and sorrow, poor health, sicknesses, and diseases. Stress is the number one cause of illnesses. And fear is the primary source of negative stress. Also, according to the Heart Mind Institute: Acute stress is the leading cause of sudden death especially in young healthy people with no evidence of coronary disease. Accept all things, resist nothing, and live contentedly; it's the way to being stress-free.

A report in the Malaysian Journal says: "The morbidity and mortality due to stress-related illness are alarming. Emotional stress is a major contributing factor to the six leading causes of death in the United States: cancer, coronary heart disease, accidental injuries, respiratory disorders, cirrhosis of the liver and suicide. According to statistics from Meridian Stress Management Consultancy in the U.K, almost 180,000 people in the U.K die each year from some form of stress-related illness. It is, therefore, necessary to rid stress from our lives. Do not worry about yourself! Says, Jesus the Christ. Make a decision to come into union with the Truth; it is the greatest anxiety reliever.

So, the union of thought and emotion is what changes our reality. Our thoughts, belief, and feelings fashion our world---this is real prayer. Consequently, if thoughts, beliefs, and feelings are fear motivated; anger, frustration, discouragement, fatigue, etc. The thing you fear will also manifest, regardless of what you are praying. Four- Believe that you have what you are desiring. A belief of any kind is your reality. E.g., if you feel you cannot, you absolutely will not. Unless, you change your thinking about yourself, your capability, abilities, and possibilities. If you believe you can, then it is very likely that you will. Believe and not doubt in your "heart," says Jesus. The human heart produces the largest field of energy humanly possible. This expanse of energy influences and rearranges our world around us. Love, gratitude, joy, and peace, etc., creates the strongest energy in the heart. Scientists are saying if we can change our feelings about a situation or condition, we can change our reality.

Accept that all things are as they should be. Favorable functioning for our welfare according to God's design. Accepting this as being so, then, of course, everything is as we believe. The universe will harmonize with your belief. Whatsoever you bind on earth is bound in heaven, and what you loose on earth is loosed in heaven (Matt.18:18.) Believing in the heart is to accept what you think as your reality and reacting accordingly to it. In fact, this is a feeling of having the reality you desire immediately. Thus, is the way to pray without ceasing, having and maintaining an attitude of consistent confidence in God's way. All things are already favorably so.

Therefore, be always mindful, giving thanks, and steadfastly assured of God's favor and loving-kindness. Maintaining an attitude in your heart that "all things are as I desire." Not focusing your thoughts on what you do not have now, but knowing, and confidently trusting--- that all that you need for this life are already in place. Nothing is absent, they are already present, and you manifest them by your attitude of; I have it now, or it is so now. The key to answered prayers is to create, and maintain a positive feeling, that "It is so," as I have prayed, so it is. Please understand this is not a concept of mind over matter, it is simply the way things are, and believing, accepting, and acquiescing to the way!

Therefore, we can justly pray knowing, as it is in heaven,

so it is on earth. Without applying any form of conditions, not thinking of any reason why it may not happen now. To judge the situation is to trigger doubts in your heart! To apply conditions is doubtfulness. Nothing can change the reality of your prayer but you. If you will believe in your heart and do not doubt you shall have what you pray. This is law!

The apostle James in his epistle says, the person who is of double minds going back and forth between belief and doubt shall not have the answer to their prayer. It is either so or not so. It is or its not---believe one! Jesus said, "believe in your heart and not doubt in your heart" that you have it as you say. In other words, express the similar feeling. Surround yourself with the emotion that will be in your heart the seat of your emotions; upon receiving your desire. That emotion is happiness---confidence, assurance and action. Do now what you would have done; when you get what you pray. Respond as though having it already!

A superb example is Elijah in the old testament---He had the desire for the end of three years of famine. Having a good motif; We know the desire is love base, of a conscious heart. He did not say Lord would you please send rain; there will be a disaster if you do not send rain soon. Elijah also did not look at the sunny skies and apply conditions why it may not happen--- to do so is doubt. Rather Elijah took on the meditative posture. He prayed or meditated and only got up from sitting or meditation when his servant returned to him with the news that he saw a small cloud---a cloud the size of a man's fist. In one day Elijah manifested "abundance of rain," ending three years of famine. We today may not have been very accepting of the servant's news; maybe we might have completely disregarded the little cloud on the horizon.

However, it was Elijah's evidence of his answer. Thus, the Prophet heard an abundance of rain! Although the rain was not yet falling, he expected a torrential downpour. Enough so, he saw it so urgently necessary to warn the king; outrunning the royal chariot.

Elijah, acted as though he already had his answered prayer. Therefore, he prepared for the dousing! It proves to the fact that we must believe we already have the answer to our prayer. Hence, feeling the emotions of already having what we've prayed. I reiterate, be happy and respond; acting as you already have your answer. You decree a thing, and it is established for you! To say, "give me," "would you please do this or that," says you do not now have your desire. Such prayer does not meet the criteria for miracles. Excitement is evidence that you will have what you say! If you believe, you will have what you say--- it will change your attitude and demeanor. It will alter the reality of it, now! As you pray, the desire is no longer a desire; but it is your new reality. Though your senses are not experiencing it, they cannot see, touch, nor feel it, but you must treat it as so!

The individual's posture must adjust in response to getting their answers now. I already have what I pray; confident, joyous, happy. The emotions are; I have it, it is so, now! Belief coupled with desire produces emotions; the feelings which impress your world; yielding your reality. It gives you the reality you want; though not yet made manifest. Thus, causing a response of happiness, gratitude, and joy that transcends all understanding, this is prayer. Prayer is your belief and thoughts concerning your desire, which creates a similar attitude of the thing you want. Without the attitude which says: "it is as I say!" I have not yet prayed.

In the gospel story of Lazarus for example, Jesus knowing that Lazarus had died delayed four days before going to Mary and Martha the sisters of Lazarus, his friend. When he arrived, the people were mourning, and Jesus was grieved in His heart. The Bible says, "Jesus wept!" Seemingly he cried not for his friend--- but because of the people's lack of faith. Hence, he prayed "Father I know that you hear me always, but I pray to you for the benefit of the people standing here, that they may believe that you have sent me." After He had prayed, he called out in a loud voice "Lazarus come forth!"

He commanded the thing, and so it was established--- as he desired it, and even so, was, it manifested. Jesus had expressed a powerful emotion according to scripture, John eleven verse thirty-five say, "Jesus wept," proving his desire and belief originated in his heart and showing how much he wanted to change the heart condition of these people.

Notice a couple of keys in His attitude and prayer: *Firstly,* His confidence; "Father I thank you that you always hear me"! The knowing must be present, and as well gratitude for the answer. You must get this; it is essential to getting the answers to prayers. Be confident that you have your desire and respond to the reality of it now. Jesus knew he had his answers to prayer every time. Not because he was God or a great teacher, but because he believed and manifested all the right conditions for the answer to his prayers. He believed and was, therefore, confident that God will answer every time.

Secondly, He had the right attitude that he already had what he prayed for and responded thus with gratitude. He gave thanks to his Father for hearing. "Father, I thank you that you hear me always" He gave all credit to Heavenly

Father! And it may seem that he would have otherwise chosen not to pray aloud. He would have only commanded his desire "Lazarus come out!" His usual style of administration for his many miracles. He would only direct the thing, and it was as he said it!

Finally, he spoke his desire; he talked to the mountain so to speak. Bid the thing to be as he had desired. In this case "Lazarus come out of the grave!" Proving the necessity of speaking or decreeing his desired outcome. First, he requested the people rolled the stone away. Hence, demonstrating his expectations of Lazarus coming out of the grave, not dead but alive. He cannot live in grave clothes--- his life must be a full and profitable one. Hitherto, Jesus commanded them, "loose him!" Is it possible for us to receive only a partial manifestation of the answers to our prayers because we are not mindful?

Praying and not expecting. That is like deciding to build a house and quitting at the finishing touches. Never bothering to finish the floors; neither tiles nor carpet are in place. No paint on the walls nor curtains in the windows. All the worst is doing everything but not possessing; not moving into the house! I have seen time and time again, people are in desperate situations and needing prayer requested I pray for them. The thing is when they have received their answer they will credit the answer to another source. They have all sort of reasoning once out of the predicament, never the source. Some will never update me on the way things have turned out, or even say thank you. Gratitude to the Divine Source is important.

Gratitude will bring about wholeness---the lack of thankfulness of itself says there is a larger problem. The problem of ingratitude will disqualify favor from the life.

Explicitness is necessary to answered prayers." If you would say to this mountain", says Jesus "be removed and be cast into the sea!" We are here instructed to speak explicitly to the problem---the undesirable condition. Say unto the mountain---tell it where to go; specifically directing its course. Justly, one should be mindful against speaking negatively or contrary concerning their lives circumstances. Praying one thing but speaking another thing is not acceptable. That is double mindedness. Be well adjusted; "I have what I pray" must always be the spirit or attitude. Do not speak or think of what you do not want in your life. For as a man thinks so is he.

It is not a surprise to me that Mr. Donald Trump is the president of the United States of America. You see President Trump knows how to keep people talking and focusing all energies on himself. The focus attention of the world right or wrong is what have positioned him in the office of President. I do not think there had been a moment when Mr. Trump thought he would not become President. It is imperative that we adjust our thoughts, to the way we want things to be--- accepting it as so already! Celebrate, this is faith the substance of the thing you have hoped.

Make the necessary changes in your life to accommodate the answer! Supposing someone is praying for workplace promotions, but are entertaining all sorts of negative thoughts, such as: "no one at work cares for them, and everyone is trying to set them up to fail." If this person always thinks negatively about their situations, of course, those are the conditions that will be present. They will not be happy and will draw another unhappy person to them, and as well more reasons to be miserable. Misery loves company! Thinking that no matter how hard they try people will sabotage their efforts. That is what will keep on manifesting in that person's work life. They will work very hard and maybe will even do a better job than many, but they will never see their rewards. In fact, others doing much less may experience much greater benefits. Even at the point of recognition, there will be sabotage. That individual will not have the favor and influence in the workplace as they may have otherwise--- if only they had a positive workplace attitude.

If you are desiring marriage and is praying for a husband or a wife, you must see or picture that spouse, what she or he looks like, imagine you are married and living together in your home. Having your meals together etc. Prepare your mind, body, and spirit to take on the role of a spouse. Read books and develop. Work on your finances and plan for your home. Buy furniture, and other necessities to give yourselves the type of life you desire, with your spouse. Make yourself ready, and create space in your life for your partner. Positively think on it--- deliberately maintaining the right thoughts. Do not be critical, believe and hold to your expectation. Be super excited, sleep on it--- the last thing you think of each night. First thing as you come into consciousness in the morning. Very soon you shall have your miracle spouse. Just recently I instructed a good friend concerning this. Telling him exactly as I am saying to you. Having joined several dating sites and found they were a waste of money and time. He was desperate for a change. In as little as a couple of weeks, the best date of his life showed up. Now when my friend speaks, I can hear the smile in his voice. Wedding bells are going to ring for these two!

Remember always the words of the proverbs "As a man

thinks in his heart, so is he!" If you are praying for your healing, you cannot be feeding your mind with evidence of the sickness. Do not be engaged or consumed by the thoughts of the illness. Our thoughts inform our beliefs, and our beliefs inform our words; which in turn will fashion our world. The words we speak can empower or defeat. Someone may ask, "how are you doing?" In this instance, your reply should be, "I am well!" activating the power of healing in your life. It is not a lie; it is as you are believing; It is already so. And do not think you should give an explanation. Neither do not speak of the sickness to anyone. By necessity choose always to speak right words. Especially that of God's truth concerning the situation. Speaking of your desire as though you already have what you have prayed for---fill your heart with joy and thanksgivings.

For as the Heavenly Father had said: As the snow falls from the sky and the rain falls to the ground and does not return. But it waters the ground that it may bring forth food for the sower and bread unto the eater. Even so said he, His word shall not return unto Him unaccomplished, but it shall prosper in the thing He purposed it (Isaiah 55:11.) This is a natural and spiritual law. God's word is programmed; empowered to accomplished as God desires. We have been created in God's image and likeness, having the power to create our worlds or lives. Our words are programmed to accomplish their purpose as we desire. Believe and speak and imagine it is so. Your words will without fail, perform as you say if you do not change your mind concerning it. You can have what you say! "If you can believe, all things are possible to him who believes, says Jesus the Christ.

Chapter Three

Believe without a doubt

Words are seeds and as such, are full of potentials. Therefore, by necessity, one must mindfully watch over their words. At all times consciously maintaining wholesome thinking and speech. Letting our words add to our lives, not take away from it. The words we speak are the direct reflection of what we believe. Our words must align with what we are praying or desiring; else it will not accomplish in our lives.

Too often we sabotage our outcome by the words we speak about ourselves and our situations. For example, people regarding their finances would say things such as, "I am so broke," "I do not have two pennies to rub together." They regularly confess "I do not have any money!" When most honestly it is that they are possibly not being mindful or grateful. What they are speaking about the circumstances must align with the change they are expecting. To speak otherwise is a violation to the way things are. Blessings and cursing proceeds from the same mouth, James says it ought not to be. Neither does bitter and sweet water flow from the same fountainhead (James 3:10). It is doubt, all that originates from fear is doubt.

It is necessary for us to understand that desiring money or anything at all, just for the sake of having it, or a lot of it makes life miserable. Such desires can never be satisfied, that individual will never have enough of it; the more they get is, the more they'll want. Hence, we should consciously determine what is the needed resource for, how does it enrich my life and that of others? Personally, I believe all resources we need to accomplish our purpose; gifts, talents, callings and vital basic needs are already available. It is about paying attention, literally being observant, gracious and thankful. You will be surprised how resources usually show up at the point of need. Desire left to itself can be like a deadly wildfire.

I have prayed many prayers for many people. People of all walks of life and I have had the privilege of observing that many people will say they believe one thing but in fact have no understanding of what they are believing. As a result, they are unstable and unsure in their desires. Their words do not support or seem to harmonize with what they believe; this is doubting.

Those who doubt will not have the answer to their prayer. Subsequently, it is essential to demonstrate control or mastery over the tongue. It is not what goes into a person that defiles him or her, but what proceeds from within. Hence, you must speak, think, and expect specifically according to the miracle you desire to see. James Allen in the book, "As a man thinks so is he." Says; The soul attracts that which it secretly wants, that which it loves, and fears. Life and death are in the power of the tongue say Proverb chapter eighteen and verse twenty-one.

Job chapter twenty-two and twenty-eight states: Thou

shalt also decree a thing, and it will be established unto thee: and the light of God shall shine upon thy ways. Stop sending mix messages or signals ---don't say one thing then do another. If you believe all resources are available, then get about it--- act! Take a leap, and do that which may move you into your actual life of purpose and riches; love, joy, and peace.

The Bible, in Psalm one hundred and twelve, says; that unto the upright there ariseth light in the darkness: He is gracious and full of compassion, and righteous. A good man shows favor and lends: he will guide his affairs with discretion. Surely, he shall not be moved for ever: the righteous shall be in everlasting remembrance. He shall not be afraid of evil tidings: his heart is fixed, trusting in the Lord. His heart is established, he shall not be afraid, until he sees his desire upon his enemies. He hath dispersed, he hath given to the poor; his righteousness endureth for ever; his horn shall be exalted with honor. The wicked shall see it, and be grieved; he shall gnash with his teeth, and melt away: the desire of the wicked shall perish.

Seek for opportunities to be compassionate, be a giver. If you indeed believe without a doubt, there are no reason to withhold from those who ask of you. The way of many people today is to take. The measure of what they receive always exceeding what they give. Scriptures teach that when we give it shall be given back to us. The thing you desire for yourself wish it for others; for as a man sows that shall he also reaps. To not do or practice what you believe is to doubt.

Where faith is, the corresponding actions will follow. Faith without works is dead says apostle James. James

Chapter two verse fourteen to seventeen thus challenges us: What doth it profits, my brethren, though a man says he hath faith, and have no works? Can faith save him? If a brother or sister be naked and destitute of daily food, and one of you say unto them--- depart in peace, be ye warmed and filled; notwithstanding ye give them not those things which are needful to the body; what doth it profits? Even so, faith, if it hath not works, is dead, being alone.

In all things, there are natural laws at work; accomplishing its purpose. For example, a farmer plants an ear of corn which yields forth a thousand times increase. He does so because he believes ultimately in a natural law of seed time and harvest. Whatever he commits to the ground shall produce after its kind.

Through faith, we understand that the worlds were framed by the word of God so that things which are seen were not made of things which do appear. Get the word of God into your affairs; what does wisdom say about your situation? Agree with what Divine wisdom says and acquiesce to it. Believe and speak essential truths as they may relate to your life and its good outcome. E.g., what the doctor say about your health may be medically the truth concerning the health of your body. But what does God say about your life? Whose word is more potent and sure? I accept and align myself with the word of God in every aspect. I believe in healing my body. I expect my complete healing all the time, and therefore I consistently see the manifestations. There is something I have observed about a personal diagnosis. I had some symptoms, regarding wish I consulted with my family doctor who ran several tests and could not find what the matter was. I as well did some research on the symptoms and concluded I had one or two autoimmune disorders, mainly Scleroderma. I went back to the Doctor, and I told him I needed more test done, and I wanted to see a Rheumatologist. My initial consult with the Rheumatologist confirmed I had Scleroderma.

The worst part is I searched for this disease and attached myself to it. Don't ever associate yourself with any sickness irrespective of the symptoms you may experience. Seek medical help yes, but do not take ownership or association with any sickness. I invited, opened and gave room to this disease in my life. Therefore, I must rid my body of it, most of the typical symptoms are gone, and I continue to expect complete healing from it. The Rheumatologist told me the other day; I am not even an ordinary patient with normal symptoms---most unusual he said. Yes, what is happening in my life and body is most extraordinary, my healing!

I will see the expression of my wholeness now! It's hard at times to maintain the correct posture necessary for the miracle healing. Consequently, we forfeit by giving the evidence or symptoms of sickness. However, I continue to believe and expect my complete healing. That does not mean that I'll disregard what the doctors say. Or would not seek their advice and treatments. Absolutely, not! They are God's workmanship; His healers in the earth. Do what you must do to heal your body. Taking medication with wisdom and mindfulness can bring about your healing. Proper attention to your health; diet, listening to your body; observing interpretive signs and responding to them appropriately. One can find their miracle on the operation table. Through the pharmacy. Through the herbalist or homeopath. I have seen a lump disappeared from the back of my hand instantaneously. By any means, healing comes it is a miracle! Everything I say to you is true, but if you do not have belief, you will not have the answer as you desire it now.

Allow yourself to believe, and be happy that your prayer is answered now. Be rightly informed on the situation in which you are dealing. Get Divine understanding as it may relate to your circumstances. If it is finance, seek the bible's truth on the matter. But also seek sound financial counsel. Do not allow ego to keep you trapped. Many times, we remain longer in unfavorable situations until it becomes a crisis. Why? We do not know how to fix or make the necessary adjustments. And we mostly do not know what to do because we choose not to speak to the people who know; and are willing to help us.

For example, you may have a problem with your mortgage payments; your first decision is to borrow some money. Borrowing to repay a debt is always temporary; Consequently, it does not work. Now instead of one debt, you have two. The mortgage plus the money you borrowed to pay the missed mortgage payment. And guess what, the next mortgage payment will soon become due again. You have more to pay than was due initially. The best thing to do in this situation is to speak to the bank's mortgage department. They have ways and means to help through these hardships situation. They may be able to rescind the past due payment for you.

Every little help is a miracle! Fix the problems before they are made worst. Become wise from your experience, now you can believe for your improved financial status. Believe and see your financial life as you desired it now; keeping your financial situation in good standing. Be happy and maintain a good feeling about your finances. Also, love others, and wish for their welfare.

Do all the things you must do, and do not forget Jesus' teaching on prayer; Believe in your heart and do not doubt, and you shall have what you pray. Surround yourself with the feeling that you have all the money, healing, or perfect family, whatever it maybe--- believe you have it already and do not doubt. Live within certain parameters, being watchful you do not encroach on God's laws. Align yourself with universal principles; agree with and do not violate one. The effectual fervent prayer of the righteous avail much!

Therefore, it is necessary for believers to Kill self or ego, the carnal man must indeed die; then and only then can one enjoy life! Why do you think the worst will happen to you, why would you be ashamed? You certainly won't, not unless you are in violation of God's laws; moral, natural, and spiritual. The word of God teaches that none who trust in Him shall be ashamed! Fears are because of wrong thinking and doubts. The ego is always creating a false reality of things.

Therefore, we need always to guard or manage our thoughts. Right now, begin to observe your thoughts what is said. Challenge what it is saying. You will observe that the voice is incessant and possesses a mind of its own. Understand that this voice is not yours, neither is the speaker you. Notice and recognize also, that there are two separate and distinctive speakers. Without a doubt, you would easily have understood that one of these voices is you; the inner you, perfect, spirit, the god you. The other is speaking to you; this is your ego--- not your real self. The conditioned, critical and judgemental you; with all external, social influences; of religion, parents, educational systems, etc.

Ego is always seeking for control, if allowed if will edge God out of your life; assuming to have the answers to your life's circumstances. However, for the most part, it is serving only to cause fear. Someone defines fear as "false evidence appearing real". Ego will tell you what people will say about you. It will tell you how bad things are, how impossible your situation is; and that there is no way out. It will also provide alternative escapes that mostly do not serve to your good.

So, it is important, critically important to discipline your thoughts. Philippians Chapter four commands that we think on whatsoever things that are true, whatsoever things are honest, whatsoever things are just, whatsoever things are pure, whatsoever things are lovely, whatsoever things are of good report. If there be any virtue, and if there be any praise, think on these things. To think otherwise is to have doubts. Every thought is a possibility for a miracle. Thoughts are very powerful; therefore, we must pay attention to what we are thinking. Become aware of thoughts and consciously choose what you think on. We design our world by our imaginations (imagery) and ideas, and create it with our thoughts! Your thoughts are as a garden; cultivate it or allow it to run wild. It will produce flowers, or it will yield weeds. A wise person builds his or her house with their hands; the foolish person destroys it with their words. Thoughts, imaginations, and words are essential to the manifestation of your daily miracles. So, take control of them; guarding both heart and tongue; thought and speech. Being mindful of what enters these faculties.

If you are going to unconsciously watch or listen to

the negatives on radio and television, indeed you will live in a certain amount of fear. These media outlets will also give you more worry or fear base messages to think on. As a matter of fact, they are always appealing to the sensory. People will ask how you get the news or know what is going on in the world? Trust me, you will know! There is not that much new news anyway. I do not have to feed my mind with television and other media outlets incessantly. There are enough people, reliable sources in my sphere to tell me anyways. But I view my news as I deem right for my involvement in my community, state, country, and the world. It is in my email, and I very consciously glance over the news highlights deciding what I should read.

I by practice do not watch television. I will look at tennis I love individual players, and they are of inspiration to me. Their focus, discipline, and determination to develop their skill. We must always vigorously and intentionally guard what enters through the gates of the eyes, ears, and mouth; they will affect your heart, mind, and thoughts. Pursue your dreams with all resolve. Never allowing lack of money and other things to hinder your pursuit; to do so is to doubt. If you think of the money that you do not have enough of it; surely you will never have enough of it. When I wrote my first book Daily Living God's Presence, I did not have the money I needed, and maybe not even the know how. However, I obeyed the command of God; knowing His provision is already available. Daily I pressed myself for about a year and published my first book.

My life is a constant prayer; every moment I live prayerfully. The expectation and gratefulness for all things are always present; all things are continually working for my good. My complete surrender is to the will and laws of God. My concerns are more for the needs of others than myself. Be an inspiration or encouragement---being mindful of the people that are present; allowing for encounters. Be purposefully in every moment; life is a miracle---don't miss any. To practice otherwise is to doubt. Being present constantly, you will soon know that no need ever goes unmet. There is always provision, every need supplied at the point of need!

I tell you again, the favor of God is always with me. Things are always working out for my good. God's favor is resident in my life. I am treated favorably on all occasions. The right persons are present to serve me as is necessary. Even as the Lord had spoken in Isaiah sixty saying, "Strangers shall build thy walls and their kings shall serve thee..." God's grace, favor, and loving kindness will be dominant in your life. Seek Him, pursue Him with your whole heart; this is the path to your fulfilled life.

Chapter Four

Believe it is all prearranged

It is all Divinely prearranged, and I understand it completely and thoroughly. Fear does not enter my heart; no, it does not exist for me. I expect certain favorable treatments, and that is what I am giving and do receive on every occasion. It is most evident in my travels; as I tend to interact with more people during these times and most things are out of my control and lies within the power of strangers.

I will get my preferred seating even when I had forgotten to reserve a seat. The cabin crew will give me more refreshment than I want. Someone will carry my heavy cowhide tote for me--- without my asking. Immigration and customs officers, I've found to be most accommodating. Especially more noticeable is when I do not have a hard copy of my returning itinerary, which is always never. I am consistently meeting and connecting with great people. Meeting my reading audience and followers are my delight. Just recently I got on a flight a thirty minutes' flight, and within five minutes in my seat, a young lady offered me her Caribbean roti, of which we; she and I each had half. I honestly was craving for roti, so I hope my drooling wasn't that noticeable. Today we are good friends. The world is a beautiful place be happy in it!

People will incessantly complain about their awful experiences with airlines, hospital's, doctors, and nurses, etc. I have never had a negative experience with any of these people, even after many, many experiences. I have a deliberate expectation, and that's what without fail influences my life's experiences. When you are mindful of all things---miracles become routine occurrences--- It will amaze you! Don't just look for the high and lofty, but observe all things, both great and small. In so doing we see much more to be grateful for, our hearts are full of joy. Thus, we are consistently happy.

I noticed a few years ago, maybe it was after I wrote the first book, Daily Living God's Presence. I only needed to have a desire, and without fail it would show up in my life! Mindfully one day I observed I had the desire for some lentil peas soup. I had left from one location to another, and within an hour of my arrival, I was served the same soup I wanted and exactly the way I like it.

The degree of which we can see or perceive our desire determines the magnitude of our manifestation.

What I mean is that our answers to prayer do not show up in our lives because of our inability to live as though the desire is already present. Also, we are not looking for or paying attention to what is already present now. Let the weak say I am strong, and let the poor say I am rich! If you so desire then "be!"

If only we would become more heedful, we will realize that we are indeed blessed beyond measures. So very often we give our attention to what others possess; thus, disregarding or taking for granted what we do have. We should rather be present, counting all that we do have and be grateful. Gratitude will magnetize your life; and will draw more good to you!

The more thankful one is, the more blessings they'll realize to be grateful. Being grateful the more compassion you will demonstrate for those that are more disadvantaged. We also need to understand that things are only as valuable as the value we place on them. That is usually proportional to our need or purpose. Things are not the most important---yet we tend to pursue with much passion. I honestly at times have felt a bit of pity for some people, because of their drive to possess things. Working doubly hard, compromisingly they crave and strive; fretful, and anxious they go about their quest for more.

There must be a value system in place; not getting things merely because others have these things. Learn and foster for yourself a life satisfying, loving, and peaceable. Thus, it will compel the blessing of God to your house. Behold how good it is for brethren to live together in harmony. Become coherent to the way God has ordained. Then you will notice that your striving is not necessary. What sense does it make killing oneself for things?

Let's say a pair of shoe is 200.00 ask yourself how long do you have to work for that shoes. Is it two hours, one-half hour or a week or two. That is the actual value of the pair of shoes. Ask yourself the question; is it worth a day or two of my life? And the same should be applied to anything. You may reason that where you are and going, you need to look the part; presenting yourself to the level of your influence now and intending to achieve. There is any amount of reasons, what price will you consciously put on anything; how much of your life are you willing to pay or exchange for a pair of shoes?

I would confess to you I do not pray for things. Have not prayed for things in years. Except for praying for someone else' need. If I am in divine will; the way as God has ordained; living my God chosen life all things are available to me. All needed resource is available to me; so that I am enabled to accomplish my tasks. People is my business, and I am God's business.

My life is rich, because of enriching other people's life. A few years or so ago I had a bit of set back financially. I had bought some lands overseas and had a rental apartment and mortgage. One month I did not have the usual payments. So, I did what I knew how to do, that's pray, to Heavenly Father. My prayer went something like this, "Father, You said I should bring my tithes into your storehouse and prove You now...," (Malachi 3:) Lord well I have given my tithes and offerings. I have been faithful to your service and work. Father, I need to prove you now, this minute, I am your responsibility, and I am waiting for You alone, my confidence is in You alone!"

Instantly, I heard a voice and a deep impression from within me said, "pick up the phone," I glanced at the phone and remained in my seat with an attitude of I do not want to speak to nobody. The voice spoke again, "pick up the phone and call _____." I thought okay, and dialed the number.

The phone rang for a while, so I figured they are not available. As I was in the process of hanging up the phone, I heard a voice on the other end said hello, hello! I brought the phone back to my ear, and I said hi, how are you? It was

_____, and immediately she said, "talk to me," but I did not say a word. So, she continued to say, "we were praying just now, and we told God we have some money and would like to use it to be a blessing to someone, and He should reveal the person to us. She continued to say when the phone rang; we were finishing our prayers." I started to cry as she further asked me, "how much do you need;" on that same night, she brought the needed money and a little more.

There is another side to this story, and it is amazing. It was just a couple of weeks prior someone came to me saying they had received an eviction notice and needed to borrow some money to pay the court. My rent was all I had so I gave it. Consequently, I could not meet my payment and was given the money by someone else. About two weeks after this, I received an offer for a property I had which exceeded my expectations. Making a good profit on the sale, I could purchase another property. That person has never repaid me that money to this day. Nevertheless, God is good!

When God and His people become our priority; our affairs become His priority. He will not abandon His own. Focused your life on being a blessing; being charitable. Making the needs of the less fortunate a priority. Choose to be content in whatever state you are in; in little or much. I have come to a place of maturity that I will give two hours or more of my life up-lifting, and teaching individuals who cannot pay me a cent than to purchase a pair of shoes for 300.00 for myself. As a matter of Fact, I will give it to someone's need than to give in exchange for a pair of shoes. Time invested in pointing someone on their way; directing them on the path of Christ is well worth it. That is indeed a worthy investment--- dividends are priceless and eternal.

I have never felt richer than when I give, and what I truly need shows up most favorably. We all do not have the same necessary needs. As a teacher, I by priority need more books, than I do more clothes or shoes and the like. You decide your priorities.

Everything will move; shift and position to accommodate. Love for God and the acceptance of His 'way" will always compel our more than abundant to us.

You were born with potential, goodness, trust, ideals, dreams, greatness and wings. You are not meant for crawling; you have wings learn to use them, fly! ~Rumi

Chapter Five

Believe you will possess what you see

I have observed in my life and life in general that we have more than we are aware. Simply put, we are richer than we think. We do not believe that we already have enough. Hence the striving---trying to get and to get more; bigger and better! There seems to be an absent of contentment and gratitude. But then again, how can someone be grateful for something they do not know that they already have? That's the problem; People do not know what or how much they have. Completely unaware of what is theirs. It is present, but they are not possessing.

Seeing is believing, but in fact, quite the opposite is true concerning prayer. Rather, believing is seeing! Whatsoever, you can imagine you will see with your natural eyes; thus, you will possess.

The ability to see holds a spiritual connotation. To see is to understand. Understanding being the eyes from which one sees; therefore, having the knowledge regarding the thing ---you do not doubt its ability to work for you. For example, you do not fly an aircraft, neither have you built one; Yet you believe and trust enough to travel at an altitude of about 51,000 feet for several hours. Your confidence is therefore based on the information you've received, understood, and believe.

Belief is necessary, as a matter of fact, it is very crucial to our life's success! It is the difference between those who succeed and those who fail. What you believe you supernaturally become! The Bible in John chapter One and verses twelve says that unto them that "believe" He give the power to become sons of God. It is true, both spiritually as well as naturally. Belief will power and draw life's possibilities to us. Isaiah eleven verses one to nine says, (the emphasis is on verse three.)

"He shall make him of quick understanding... He shall not judge by the sight of His eyes..." In other words, we will not judge the situation on what we see, or what appeals to the senses; but by what Divine wisdom has revealed. When we have the right understanding on any matter that we are praying, there are no conditions or judgments. Rather we are surrendered to the truth of the Divine. We see clearly, believing and responding according to the God's truth. Therefore, we have freedom from conditions.

There is an influential power that comes by way of spiritual understanding. If you were to look at the parable of the sower, (Matt. 13:1-23, Mark 4:1-20, and Luke 8:1-15.) The difference there is the level of understanding. The sown seed of the word could not withstand the test. Satan's primary strategy in tempting us is to cast doubt, "Did God say...?", "If you be the Son of God...!" If we do not understand and know the laws and way of God, we are going to waver or doubt. Understanding is, therefore, the difference between us having happy lives and fulfilled destiny.

Understanding of truth is what brings about conviction. Belief fuels passion, passion is what gets you moving. The wrong thing can drive you. It is possible to have an understanding based on a lie, and convicted of something, not at all accurate; yet is passionate about it. The result not at all desirable. However, when you have a thorough understanding of the truth, and is convicted and moved, acting on the truth you are powerful. "You shall know the truth, and the truth shall make you free" (John.8:32).

The understanding of the truth will determine your level of power! Understanding will also eradicate doubt and uncertainty. An individual who doubts he or she will have the answer to their prayer will certainly not get what they pray; the person must believe. It is the effectual fervent prayer of the righteous (One in alignment with the Divine.) which avails much says James in chapter five and verse sixteen. If you are asking me for something but you are not certain of what you're asking me for, how then can I give you what you need? Therefore, be specific about what you are praying. As well, you must know and believe without a shadow of a doubt that your source is able and willing to grant your desire.

Only then will you have the assurance that you will get what you are asking. Without the guarantee, you more than likely will have doubts. James says the individual who doubts is like the waves of the sea (James1:6-7.) Doubting, uncertain, and unstable; going back and forth! This moment they're decided, and in the next moment they are not; just like the sea, forever swaying and turning.

Wavering or doubting is more than likely because of lack of understanding concerning the circumstance. Lacking, confidence in your relationship with the Source or your source. If there are doubts as it relates to an individual's relationship with God, one will most certainly be unsure of His willingness to support them. Therefore, like Adam and Eve, they try to cover their wrongs and hide from God. No one can run nor hide from God. Neither can we solve the problem of ours and His relationship alone and on our own.

Knowing the truths of who God is to you and who you are to Him is of vital importance. Also, understanding who He is and His Divine nature. If you do not personally know the love and grace of God concerning you in this instance, you need to gain an understanding of who He is, and experience Him now. Become acquainted with His character and His word as it relates to what you are experiencing. Put the word of God on the issue, know His truths, and believe and trust His promises. None that trust in Him shall be ashamed. He resists the proud, but He gives grace to the humble.

Be humbled to believe that without Him one can do nothing. Believe, all good things are sent from heaven above--- from the heart of God. Believe, all things are of Him, and He can do exceeding and abundantly above all we can ask or think. The believer is in Christ--- in God, and nothing is impossible for they who believe and confidently put their trust in Him.

Understanding is light upon an otherwise dark path. It is the light that reveals; correcting faulty concepts and ideas. The psalmist David penned in Psalm twenty-three and verse one, "The Lord is my shepherd I shall not want." The believer has no lack---he is truly satisfied. You are richer than you think!

Chapter Six

Believe dreams do come true.

Children are especially the best at dreaming. They typically naturally live by their imagination. From anywhere they can get there! Live in places, rule over lands, travel around the world in a flash--- talk with angels and defeat monsters. All accomplished through imagination.

Until they are amalgamated into the world's way of rush, rush, hurry; which teaches to retaliate against dreams and dreamers. Dreams are insignificant and dreamers idle time wasters. Just recently I overheard a parent saying to her son; "come-on stop your day dreaming--- pay attention!" We, adults, need to learn from the children. Maybe she should have allowed the child to daydream for a time, allowing for the much needed intellectual and emotional stimulation. Then she may try to accomplish her intended goal. Adults have, to our detriment unlearned to imagine or daydream.

Seeing is believing, this can be very true if and only if one can see beyond the physical or natural. If you can imagine, visualize and be convicted in your heart by what you see; you will have what you see or believe. We have become a culture of people who do not deliberately dream. People are not visualizing, nor imagine their lives full of their desires. When was the last time you lived your life exactly as you wished it? A quote of Douglas H Everett says, "There are some people who live in a dream world, and there are some who face reality, and then there are those who turn one into the other."

Dream your dream; you are well on your way to it being your reality. Image---imagine the life you desire, and you shall have it. The only person to prevent you is yourself; only you can stop your dreams. Greater is he that is in you than he that is in the world. Rid yourself of all the doubts, fears and judgments; that says you can not, it cannot work, etc.

Many people think that it is pointless to daydream. Consequently, their inner yearnings go unmet, and their dreams unrealized; overcome by a false sense of satisfaction. Living each day unfulfilled and unhappy; especially when left alone to themselves. When the party or conference is over, and they must face the inner self alone, thinking it easier to ignore, they have chosen to adopt to unfulfillment. Allowing lack, fear of the unknown, and skeptics to hinder them from seeing their dreams. You cannot afford to settle for less. Believe it and live it every day, soon you will realize that you must be it! Then you will create the opportunity for its realization. The opportunity will come, look for it or create it.

Self-motivation is key to accomplishing a purpose. You choose, it is in your power to choose. Create your destiny---your life is a miracle realize it! Everybody you know will not necessary understand your vision or even want you to succeed. It is tough and may get very frustrating, especially when those closest to you are not your cheerleaders. Too bad, choose to dream anyway, and do all that you must to bring about your fulfillment.

No person can take you where they have not themselves gone. If they cannot see or imagine themselves, how can they perceive or assume you being who you are to be? To be surrounded by people that are unrealized can serve to frustrate dreamers and visionaries. They can cause you to doubt your possibilities.

These used to be quite a frustration for me. For a very long time, I thought people did not understand me. As a result, I spent an endless amount of energy on explaining myself. Burdened by the notion that people are not getting me and my vision. Until I came to the realization, most people would not easily adapt to my vision. How can they? If they, for the most part, cannot imagine or have a vision for themselves. On the other hand, as well they may not even want to support my dream.

A couple, of times I have wanted to do certain things and felt I was not getting the support I needed; as a result, I did not exercise the idea. I have observed that after some time had elapsed others were doing the same thing, my idea, doing what I should have done, and are having the success that should have been mine; if only I would have persisted. Please hear me beloved---you must embrace your creative possibilities "now" today--- at this moment, or someone else will do it! Ideas are time sensitive.

Your idea is your genius seeking opportunity now. Believe in yourself and create your opportunity! Some folks typically do not have thought that is originally their own.

Every idea or thought or concept is that of someone else. Therefore, understand that if the people in your sphere do not believe their possibility--- they more than likely will not think or imagine yours. So, it is critical for you to surround yourself with people of like mind or spirit. Call on the folks you admire, and ask them to mentor you. By law two cannot walk unless they agree. One thing I have personally experienced; is that the right people will come.

Associate with people who have been there; where you are trying to get. Have done what you want to do. Your greatest assets now are friends that are not afraid of your accomplishments and want to see you succeed. Why? For one: they will celebrate you, which will, in turn, empower you to accomplish your goals further. "Keep away from people who try to belittle your ambitions. Small people always do that, but the great make you feel that you, too, can become great." ~ Mark Twain

You must also celebrate other people. The more you celebrate others, the more you are as well celebrated. What you want that you should give also. Possess a positive attitude in all things; having a positive outlook on life. Be excited about life, life is good, and the world is a beautiful place; it is not all gloom and doom. The devil is not always fighting you! Rid your life of the humbug fear; judgment, criticism, bitterness, resentment, distrust, grudge, strife and striving, etc. Develop yourself in love; consciousness, compassion, empathy; caring, giving and the like.

Exercise your gifts and callings; doing what you love and loving what you do. Your dream and your gift are connected. Think of the thing you desire and wish you could do right now. Do you often daydream about doing this thing, and does it arouse excitement in you? Are you excellent at it; but being excellent at it is not vital at this point. Will it bring you fulfillment and joy whether you make money from it or not; and will it enrich your life and that of others?

If you've answered yes, why then aren't you moved toward fulfilling it? Henry David Thoreau says, "If one advances confidently in the direction of one's dreams, and endeavors to live the life which one has imagined, one will meet with a success unexpected in common hours." Believe in your dreams and be moved to action!

The ability to visualize is vital to have the answers to your prayers. God demonstrated this with Abram. Abram needed a Child and had so prayed for a son and heir. God had also promised to make of him a great nation. However, years went by, and his wife never brought forth a child. One night God visited Abram and took him out of his tent. He had Abram to look to the sky, and He asked him this remarkable question: "can you count the number of stars in the heavens?"

Abram needed his imagination stimulated, therefore was he removed from his familiar and limited space. The four walls which restricted his vision, and the people who could not perceive him. He could not picture such greatness of which God had promised. The idea of which amused even his wife Sarah---it was to her an impossibility; merely somewhat of a laughing matter. The creator knew the power of a dream, and that you can have what you can see within; though it may not now exist. Thus, taking Abraham outside of his tent he asked him, "Can you count the number of stars in the sky? Following this rhetorical question; was the resounding words; "So shall your seed be." (Gen.15:5) Reaffirming His promise of Genesis twelve and verses one to three.

Imagination creates all things, that is the way things are. God knew if Abraham could see by imagination and thought he would believe; and as a result, there will be change to his reality. His seed will, therefore, be numberless; according as God promised. Believing he is "father of many nations;" a "son" therefore is no longer a long shot. I think that from that moment Abraham saw things as though he had his promise already. Abraham, I believe at some point became fixated with the heavens.

He may have developed a fondness for the outdoors. There he can dream---seeing himself as the great nation God had promised. Seeing, he had not yet held his son---I believe upon every opportunity Abraham was seen gazing into the sky. Fixated on doing the impossible thing of counting the stars. Counting to a few hundred, and then to start all over from one again and again. By this, he understood and grew more and more ecstatic. The promise though so great, in time, had a profound possibility. He saw his seed as the countless numbers of stars in the sky. Subsequently, Isaac became for him a matter of a dream away!

Belief coupled with visualization is key to answered prayer. Don't just pray, live your prayer daily---see what you pray and you shall see it even as you have desired. Dream your dream see it in all its details. It is possible, and thus the path to your fulfillment and destiny. Therefore, you cannot afford to ignore. Until you can understand who you are and can interpret yourself to the world, you will never be truly happy or fulfilled. Know who you are and what is your gift (s). There is a room or place prepared for you, your seat, your position and no one can take it from you! "Start where you are. Use what you have. Do what you can." Says Arthur Ashe.

Your gifts will make room for you. Exercise it constantly without fail. Give it your all, your best at every opportunity, be relentless. Work on perfecting that gift! You will soon find it is becoming the best. Every day you exercise your gift it is becoming the best of your best. It will bring you to your place or seat of prominence---your destiny! Similarly, was the story of Joseph's life; found in Genesis chapter forty-one. His gift made room for him and brought him into the presence of the King the pharaoh. In that instance, he was given the position of Governor; because he was the best at what he did. He was the best at interpreting dreams and giving wisdom solutions. Joseph was the man with the plan--- he had the answer to the king's problem. (Gen. 41.)

There is someone who can benefit from your gift and is willing to pay for it. Is it a song? Compose or sing it. If it is a book, then write it. Is it a word--- say it loud and clear! Thousands need to hear it. That can be through reading a book. Through a song, an individual can be given hope, or inspiration to get up and go again. There are miracles connected to your gifts!

Back in 2009 when I was writing my first book "Daily living God's Presence" There was a show airing called "Britain got talent" I heard about it from a friend, who told me about this female contestant. She gave me the competitor's name and insisted I watched it! I looked at the episode on youtube and quickly realized the amazement. The candidate certainly did not look the part. Oh no, not according to the pop culture.

According to our biases, she should not have even bothered, just because of her appearance. To the audience; all who were watching--- she did not fit into that mold. I remember many in the audience, even the panel of Judges seemed to spurn at her. However, when the 48 years old Susan Boyle opened her mouth to sing her song, "I dreamed a dream" it was most electrifying. Everyone shocked beyond belief! Even now I am compelled to listen again to Boyle's "I Dreamed a Dream." The tears still flow!

In her interview before her performance, she admitted to being scared when asked if she was scared; but she had always wanted to be a singer. She said, "I have always wanted to sing to a large audience, and I am going to make that audience rock!" Scared or not, she knew this was the opportunity of a lifetime, and she will not allow anything to get in the way of her being her dream. Destiny begins in the moment dream encounters opportunity.

Susan gave the guys behind the curtains a thumb up, and the music started. Everyone held their breath fearing the worst for her. Ms. Boyle parted her lips almost effortlessly, and jaws dropped, complete astonishment filled the room and airwaves! What she did, was my inspiration to finishing my first book. Actively guard your dreams and do not allow anyone to subvert them. Susan could have allowed the air of doubt to discourage and hence sabotage her opportunity.

However, she remained inspired and focused. Consequently, she realized her destiny. Her first album, I Dreamed a Dream released in November 2009. It was a huge hit, selling over a million copies in six weeks, and topping charts in the United States and the United Kingdom. A year later, in November 2010 Boyle released a Christmas album titled The Gift. The Gift also soared to the No. 1 spot on U.S. and U.K. charts.

I have always wanted to be a spiritual teacher and writer; therefore, to this end have I been employing myself in both, even from my youth. Teaching being my Divinely ordained and chosen path. Today, I am "being!" "To Be is to do;" "to do is to be;" "do be, do be--- do!" These are words of ordinary yet great men. Average individuals who chose to be and do something by publicizing their idea or concept. One man initially wrote "To be is to do" on a bathroom wall. That followed by another who wrote next to it "To do is to be" and the latter you may recognize as the words of the great singer Frank Sinatra, "do be, do be--- do!" You are great--- dare to "be" do; do you! "Be" the miracle you are desiring, someone is looking, longing and waiting for their miracle. You may be that needed inspiration!

I was on the verge of giving up--- writing my first book. Susan Boyle had been that inspiration I needed in that critical moment. She was my inspiration---my miracle! Even so, has my book been a great source of encouragement and inspiration to many? And If it had blessed only one person, it would have been worth my not giving up. Today I am the miracle to someone's dream--- Here is your miracle!

The belief that changes our reality is without conditions, biases, and judgments. Our conditions, perceptions, and preferences concerning things and how they are--- is a major impediment to our dreams. Let us do an experiment: Think of your gift and how much you want to practice it. Now make the decision to do something about it. If it is singing, consider booking a studio for a recording. Think of whatever you can do to showcase your gift. Have a concert. Think big and outside the box!

Observe that to everything you think of there is that voice finding all sorts of reasons you cannot or should not.

Notice again, listen to the voice, is this you? No, it is not you; it is your ego trying to protect itself. The more you listen in on its conversation, the more it talks. In fact, I believe that what the ego is saying is your conditioning; through socialization and personal experiences. You must learn to observe these conditions, judgments, and biases it has of you, others and all things. They will hinder your dreams from materializing. Views and conditions such as these are excellent, and that is bad. I do not have money. Who will help me? I do not have enough education. My family is not recognized enough. On and on.

Biases: If she could not do it with all the money they have. It is who know you, not who you know! I know so many people who tried that and failed. You just can not, who do they think they are? Be aware of these humbugs and rid them of your thoughts.

Practice to turn down your ego consciously. Eventually, it will do less talking. But be mindfully watchful. It desires to control and will rise soon again. Deliberately shut it up by doing the opposite of its suggestions.

The world is full of very talented and inspiring people of whom it was said--- they could not, or should not. Or may have had a difficult time of making their dreams reality. One of my favorites and very inspiring is Edison; he maybe holds the record for most failed. Having failed several thousand times before inventing the functional light bulb. His response thus most infamously inspiring to countless many: "I have not failed; I've just found ten thousand (10,000) ways that won't work." Most of us are aware of Ms. Oprah Winfrey's story. The life challenges she faced and overcame. Her struggles would have destroyed many others.

Also, too are the countless many who were told no and had the doors slammed in their faces. Would you believe Stephen King's first work rejected some thirty times? Michael Jordon also; dismissed by coaches who considered him too short. Mr. Jordon is in the NBA Hall of Fame. The greatest of Prophets, teacher, and reformers endured great cruelties. These people regardless of the oppositions faced continued to believe in their calling and purpose.

Believing in their "is-ness"; being who they "are." Doing their best repeatedly until the right moment in time came; when dream met with opportunity and destiny hatched. We see them now after the ugliness; after people's disbelief, after the no(s), insults and turn downs, and we are amazed! Be that amazement; you are "that," dream---dare to dream!

Joseph's dream was to govern; this was also his Divine chosen path. As well interpreting dreams were his gift; demonstrating that he was a sagacious man. He saw himself ruling long before he became governor of Egypt. (Gen.37) Your dream will attract the wrong people; the haters and most certainly the absolute right ones. Those whose desire it is to kill you and abort your dream. As well as those who would celebrate you and talk about you to the right people. Individuals who will introduce you to the right people, those with the power to position you!

I tell you this; there is a spot, position and seat with your name on it, be whom you are called to be. Destiny is calling your name; you are next--- the next great writer, next great songwriter, great teacher, the extraordinary musician, exceptional leader, and so much more! Do not ever give up on your dream! "Dreams do come true." says John Updike "Without that possibility, nature would not incite us to have them."

"You are never too old to set another goal or to dream a new dream."
~C.S. Lewis

Chapter Seven

Believe your possibility is limitless

Thinking back to my childhood--- being under the charge of my parents. Whatsoever I needed they gave it to me. Even those things I did not even imagine having needed. For those things I needed I accessed, I part-took as was necessary for me. And the things that were not as readily accessible to me I asked them. Sometimes I had to wait, other times it was given immediately. All in all, I could have trusted my parents to be favorable in providing for me. Guess what; they are humans having their many natural limitations.

Jesus' teaching in Matthew chapter seven verse eleven says, "If ye then, being evil, know how to give good gifts unto your children, how much more shall your Father which is in heaven give good things to them that ask him?" Most people are not aware of how much they do have. Being completely unaware to their blessings they are so very unappreciative and worrisome. The key to thankfulness is awareness. Being awaken to what we have now---what is already ours. There will be gratitude. As a matter of fact, thankfulness is a choice. We can choose to be grateful; there are so many reasons to be thankful. Be grateful for it, and do not covet what others have. Live in the moment thankfully.

I have said before; gratitude will magnetize your life, and draw your desires to you! Fighting and clawing for individual material things are not necessary. Be actualized, know who you are personally; in spirit and truth. I ask you who are you? Knowing who you are and how you can apply yourself in service to others--- or the world, and your world. That moment you are awakened, to knowing who you are in spirit, and would be moved by this knowing. The universe will begin to shift and to align with you.

One must first be moved inside before change can occur on the outside. The "way" is the path to love, peace, and joy---the kingdom. Jesus said the kingdom is within. The kingdom of God is not food, meat nor drink but righteousness. Peace and joy in the Holy Spirit. So, stop the striving, and trust your heavenly Father. For He can do exceeding and abundantly above that which you can ask, think or imagine (Ephesian 3:20.) Anything you can ask, think or imagine Divine Source can do. God will outperform every time.

As for me personally, my life is a prayer, I live each day meditatively. Constantly being aware of what is going on about me. I live in absolute knowing that whatsoever I need are already provided. They are mine I do not fight the devil for them; Christ has already accomplished that victory.

Only I can forfeit that; if I compromise and transgress the laws of the kingdom of God and or the moral laws. For each of this principle produces their consequences. Accordingly, I rest confidently in that knowledge with all gratefulness. That does not mean I do not have challenges, maybe more than others, but the difficulties are not my focus. I know soon they will be over and behind me. I give my attention only to what the challenge is accomplishing for me. Doing what I must and fix my posture according to my desired outcome and that's it. I am greater than my circumstances!

By principle, I do not borrow or spend beyond the cash, I have in hand. Am guided by spiritual, moral and natural life principles, which work for me every time. Giving and it is given back to me pressed down shaken together and running over; men gives into my bosom. It is not always that I can give monetarily. Nor do I always receive monetarily. Whatever of what I have I give willingly and cheerfully. Of time, wisdom; a kind word, or encouragement. A listening ear or a prayer of comfort. A loving embrace, or a complement to a stranger on the street. There are so many ways in which to sow good seeds. These are always producing an hundred-fold.

Know that in all things planted it is God who gives the increase. He supplies in abundance; beyond what is seeded. That is the nature of God; He consistently, exceeds expectations and imaginations. He endlessly goes over the top for us. He will blow your mind every single time---- you cannot out ask, imagine or out think Him! In Genesis chapter eight verse twenty-two the Bible says, as long as the earth exists, seed-time and harvest, cold and hot, summer and autumn, day and night will not cease. This law is perpetual; what you sow that shall you also reap. Also, whatever you plant can only produce of the same. All things will reproduce of its kind. When good is sown, ultimately good is harvested.

Can any of you by worry add an inch to your stature? Asked Jesus, since you cannot do this very little thing, why do you worry about the rest? (Matt. 6:27) You must quit from worrying; worry causes stress in our lives. Anxiety declines our life's quality. Stress is now the number one killer; due to stress, related illnesses brought on by fear and worry. In verse twenty-eight, Jesus continued to say, "Consider how the wild flowers grow. They do not labor or spin. Yet I tell you, not even Solomon in all his splendor was not dressed like one of these. If that is how God clothes the grass of the field, which is here today, and tomorrow is thrown into the fire, how much more will he clothe you---you of little faith!

My definition of Little Faith is thus: possessing enough faith to be curious, but not enough to believe and surrender to the way of Christ. Not enough belief to change perceptions and concepts of the way things are. The old world has come to an end---it has passed way! "And it is easier for heaven and earth to pass," said Jesus in Luke sixteen and verses seventeen. "than one tittle of the law to fail." There is a new paradigm which now exists with me and countless others of this modern era. Because of our knowledge and belief what took former generations years to achieve is taking us, my generation of believers a vast less the amount of time.

The things of earth; all that pertains to this life are already given to humankind. We have dominion authority now. Over the earth, sea, and air. So, we command things, such as money and other tangibles. They are ours; all these are possible to those who believe. We have dominion over all things; henceforth we can effect change upon our worlds.

According to the gospels, Peter and other disciples of

Jesus had fished all night yet caught nothing. So being completely spent, they decided to wash their nets; and quit fishing for the time! But Jesus said unto them "cast your nets on the other side!" These were experienced fishermen. I believe that for just a moment they may have questioned Jesus' command. Or were they so desperate for a catch that they very quickly tossed their nets out again? Regardless they obeyed Jesus' command and as a result caught more fish than their nets could handle. The fish was too much; they had to call for other fishers to join in on the catch.

Herein is an example of life without limits; Jesus demonstrated that we have dominion power and authority over systems. Over every creeping thing, fowl of the air and the fish of the sea as well as the beast of the fields. Genesis chapter one and verse twenty-six says, "And God blessed them, and God said unto them, be fruitful, and multiply, and replenish the earth, and subdue it: and have dominion over the fish of the sea, and over the fowl of the air, and over every living thing that moves upon the earth." Even so had God gave human dominion authority. It once forfeited through humanity's fall is reclaimed by Christ's death, resurrection, and ascension.

The universe is in alignment with you; you can decree a thing, and it will be so for you! Accept Dominion authority, submit to it, and the same power will also become the power within you. In the gospels, the disciples of Jesus had asked him to teach them how to pray. According to their request, he said to them; say "Our Father who is in heaven hallowed be thy name thy kingdom come thy will be done on earth as it is in heaven. Give us this day our daily bread and forgive us our debts as we forgive our debtors. For thine is the kingdom the power and the glory forever" (Matt.6:11.)

However, this translation is said or believed by certain scholars to be a departure from what Jesus had spoken. They teach the original text or the ancient text as being: "Our Father who is in all of us or all people." Would this version not affect you in a more powerful way? If God is only in heaven, it points to disconnection, distance, and separation. Let's be real; prayer is challenging for these very reasons. So many people see God as being out there somewhere; distant, far off and absent. Many as a result see Him as unreachable. Prayer is seeming to be such a long shot! But the reality or truth that Heavenly Father is in me. He may be in heaven, okay, but by His Omnipresence, He indwells us and is with us always. God is in you, me and everyone! Not only within, but He is all around and with us!

I have told you before of my revelation up on the hill. Mainly that space is full of massively powerful energy. God is incredibly enormous power; substantially high intelligence and exceeding vast powers. The same energy outside of me is me---I am of the same high energy. I am, you are, that same high energy, and all things are intense energy. In Him, I live, and move and have my being.

Right now, at this moment I decree that your heart/mind will undergo a shift--- changing your life and world. That as you believe and obey the "way" of God as He reveals to you. The scales of blindness will fall from your eyes, right now it is so! An endless supply of peace saturates you. Right now, there is a presence of more than enough. The Abundance that Christ gives fill your life now--- right now it is so, already so! Your days of limitations and just enough is over. Now, you have fresh and abundant supply, where you once lack!

Your life is now such that you must invite others to share in your abundance, your overflow. By their association and kind-heartedness towards you--- they are blessed! What you have toiled so hard for, and have desired so long, is happening now. Suddenly, the answer to almost forgotten prayers! You are limitless, as vast as is Universe!

Jesus taught by the power of imagination all the time. His style of teaching he utilized to get his followers to think outside the box. Challenging them to see beyond the obvious. To see passed the natural, to what is present, what "is!" Things are not so because you believe them to be so. They are so simply because that is the way things "are;" how it "be"! It is critical for you to understand me clearly. There is a "being" to all things, and it is the way Divine intelligence had designed and ordained. The way God has created all things. They are not so because you are saved, your religion or lack thereof makes no difference in this. It is so, and that is all to it. Of course--- those who know their God shall do exploits. They shall without a doubt experience His good favor and loving-kindness, all who put their trust in Him. As a matter of fact--- no one can apprehend the things of God without surrendering to who He is and His way or is-ness!

The unbeliever is not enlightened--- his eyes are blinded, and he will not see. It is as though the truth is hiding from such persons. They remain in the dark, although the command is to seek, knock and ask! Think about what I say to you, and believe how things are; Know that your desire or prayer is your reality now. Feel it in your heart, know it and move with excitement. If you believe what I am saying to you--- do them, you will begin to miraculized your life!

One need to first "believe" what is! E.g., an individual takes medicine hoping for relief or healing. Time and time again I have bought medicine, but took it only once or twice. To discontinue the dosage because I did not believe it can do what it was prescribed to do. On the other hand, there are certain drug that I think works; therefore, needing remedy I swallow the dosage and go about my day as though the pain is gone. Knowing it works, there is no reason to judge the drug or my condition. I simply accept my desired outcome.

Think about the placebo effect: a group of people is selected; The placebo group is given something and told it would heal their condition. They took the placebo as instructed and are healed; All be it by nothing but sugar! Just as powerful is the nocebo effect, individual believes for example that they will have cancer and die; because others in their family had it and they died. And so, it is as they think! Thus proving the power of thoughts, beliefs and expectations; also exemplifying a natural and Universal Laws at work in all things.

Our Beliefs, thoughts, and emotions are very powerful, and together they create our world. By our understanding, thoughts, and feelings we create wealth and good health---life more than abundant! The Word of Christ says, "The thief comes to steal to kill and to destroy, but I come that you might have life and life more abundantly." Not only eternal life to come but here and now--- He shows His "way" of life more abundantly. More than, abundance; physically, emotionally and spiritually on all levels. In this life now on earth and for all eternity with Christ!

If I were to ask you if it is in my power to give you your heart's desire right now, what would that be?

Most people would not be truthful, or they just don't know. I ask you, what can I do for you----I can give you the desires of your heart, please tell me what they are? Please be specific and to the point. Imagine each of these desires if there are more than one. Take the time to envision each, examine each to see if this is your personal and individual desire or prayer. Now, itemize your desire and add descriptions if possible. For example, to purchase my house in Northeast London. If you can include pictures or images of your wishes, beautiful. The creation is structured to respond to us in this earth. It supports us in all things we desire in our hearts. Whatever, we want persistently believing, speaking, thinking, or meditate upon is accomplished for us. We shall have.

A Shoe salesman and his family had rented a house. The house was previously rented by his mother a housekeeper. She rented the house from a wealthy lawyer, who inherited it from his mother after her death. The wealthy lawyer had other houses and did not have any use really for this small suburban home. So, he rented it to his housekeeper, telling her to pay whatsoever she could afford. She agreed to give the wealthy lawyer three hundred dollars per month. This was her earnings she would receive from the Lawyer. Thus, when she would receive her wage she would not take it, rather she would change the envelope, and leave it for the Lawyer.

She did this until she could not work anymore. And requested her son to put cash of 300 dollars in an envelope and had him dropped in the letter box at the door of her once employer. He continued this long after she was deceased. The thing is; however, the lawyer had given her the house, and asked she discontinued the rent payments. She, however, insisted on purchasing the home with the same amount, of three hundred dollars each month.

One faithful day the shoe salesman received two visitors. One appeared very astute as he strolled in carrying a briefcase and an umbrella, the other brought in a cardboard box, which he placed on the floor and quickly excused himself. The gentleman sat in the seat offered him. Opening his briefcase, he asked the shoe salesman his name and how long he lived in the house. To which he replied, for 53 years, sir; I was born here. The gentleman requested the shoe salesman to open the box which the other man had brought in. The lawyer's legal representative, further inquired if he recognized the contents in the box. The man of the house replied no sir but taking a closer look, he took an envelope in his hand, scrutinizing it he said; well, of course, I do sir. Astonishingly he replied, these are the payments for our rent. Most nervously he looked at the man, as he nonchalantly looked over the documents atop his briefcase. He said to the shoe salesman these are rent indeed. Mr. Watson never accepted any of your payments. Rather, he intended the house to go to your mother, but she refused taking it for nothing, chose instead to pay for it. These are all the payments.

Also, the shoe store on Calais Street he bequeaths to you. The same shoe store where he had worked from the age of 17. For over fifty years, rent was paid by the humble shoe salesman's mother and then by himself. He never knew the house was his. Although he daily silently wished he'd purchase the charming home one day. After he had composed himself, he said most gleefully; Every day I've lived here I dreamed and prayed; saving every little I can. Hoping, this house would one day be mine.

Your miracle is but a dream away---believe your idea, it is that potential miracle. You can exceed limits and imaginations when you believe. Know it, think it, live it, and do not doubt. No one or nothing can stop, or prevent your dream!

To accomplish great things, we must not only act, but also dream; not only plan, but also believe. ~Anatole France

Chapter Eight

More given more received

I will rebuke the devourer for your sakes, and he shall not destroy the fruits of your ground; neither shall your vine cast her fruit before the time in the field, saith the LORD of hosts.

Give, and it shall be given back to you. "...so, shall others give into our bosoms full measure pressed down and shaken together. And running over!" (Malachi 3: 10-11.) Thus, can the giver expect, preservation, and a vast supply. Many do not see these manifested in their lives because they do not believe the natural laws. Things are the way they are, whether you believe or not.

I practice this principle not only with my income or money; but in all things, I receive. Therefore, I am not Stingy about anything whatsoever. I live in the over-- flow; locked into the stream of more than enough! All that I have are gifts, not only for myself but everyone. To keep it is to violate the universal law. Whatever, we receive are bestow upon us to be shared. We are distributaries in the earth; whereby all may be blessed. To keep to oneself is to cut off others supply, and eventually oneself. Nothing is of or from us---so in principle, we must give it away. I am blessed, and daily I see the great favor of God at work in my life personally. Others are blessed and favored because of their association and favorable attitude towards me; whether they know it or not.

All the wealth I need is mine, and it is present and available to me when needed. That is not necessarily money. As needful as money is, favor is greater than money. It opens doors and opportunities which money may not be able to access. I have the all-round blessings and favor of God. I do not want you to think that life's tangibles are everything, that they are what gives one true happiness. Far from the truth. Rather, it is a chosen response to foundational truths, a deep an abiding conviction---which says It is well, despite what may be otherwise unfavorable!

All things are working for my good. Despite what is going on around me, I am not limited by what has happened, or is happening to me! I am more than my experiences! True happiness is that hidden riches of joy, peace, and love; by which one is stable despite the pain and conflicts. There is grace given; joy is present within, and hence, there remains a song in the heart.

Pope Francis says it well, "Being happy is not having a sky without storms, or roads without accidents, or work without fatigue, or relationships without disappointments. Being happy is finding strength in forgiveness, hope in one's battles, security at the stage of fear, love in disagreements.

Being happy is not only to treasure the smile, but that you also reflect on the sadness. It is not just commemorating the event but also learning lessons in failures. It is not just having joy with the applause but also having joy in anonymity. Being happy is to recognize that it is worthwhile to live, despite all the challenges, misunderstandings and times of crises. Being happy is not inevitable fate, but a victory for those who can travel towards it with your being. Being happy is to stop being a victim of problems but become an actor in history itself.

It is not only to cross the deserts outside of ourselves but still more, to be able to find an oasis in the recesses of our soul. It is to thank God, every morning for the miracle of life. Being happy is not being afraid of one's feelings. It is to know how to talk about ourselves. It is to bear with courage when hearing a "no." It is to have the security to receive criticism, even if it is unfair. It is to kiss the children, pamper the parents, have poetic moments with friends, even if they have hurt us. Being happy means allowing the free, happy and simple child inside each of us to live; having the maturity to say, "I was wrong"; having the audacity to say, "forgive me." Happiness is present because of conscious, mindfulness living. It is a life lived from the heart. The demeanor fixed on Love, Gratitude, contentment; trust is present always.

Continually observing God in all circumstances, you may go through. It does not say that you would not have unfavorable circumstances, but there is a knowing that this is only for a season--- it will pass. There is a time limit on it--- It will soon expire! You continue to hold to your confident knowing there is a season to every purpose under heaven. Not only that, but it is good for you---it is working together for your good. Therefore, it is all good!

You can, therefore, mount up. Not burdened, depressed

nor cast down by the unfavorable experience. But giving thanks in all things---the will of God is working on your behalf. Despite the opposing circumstance, be at peace and rest. Remain mindfully contented in all things on all occasions. Ralph Waldo Emerson says it so eloquently: "The purpose of life is not to be happy. It is to be useful, to be honorable, to be compassionate." We are called not to Greatness but to humility---to serve! In such contentedness, we are honored.

These are the words of The Infinite Source, our Heavenly Father: "for every animal of the forest is mine, and the cattle on a thousand hills. I know every bird in the mountains, and the insects in the fields are mine. If I were hungry, I would not tell you, for the world is mine, and all that is in it." Now, this, therefore, being Heavenly Father's attitude concerning things. Why do you or I need have another stance? We are His heirs and joint heirs with Christ! All that are His are ours. We do not have to beg for anything, all that we need He supplies. Jesus says, Knock, and the gate or door shall open unto you. Ask, and it shall be given unto you. Seek, and you shall find. We must invite, we must ask for entry and access. We must open and provide access and entrance into our hearts and lives. "Unto all that lacks wisdom let them ask of God," says the writer of James chapter one verse five--- who gives to all who ask, and He upbraids not. Ask for the things of the Spirit is the author's intent.

As it may pertain to the things of this earth, of the tangibles; we are to rejoice and give thanks! Regarding food, clothing, and the like, Jesus said in the Gospels: "Do not worry for yourself what ye shall eat or put on, for your Heavenly Father knows what things ye have need of." "Do not be as the heathen." All these and more they worry. Do not be as they are, do not be as one who does not believe! Herein he seems to imply that worry is a result of unbelief. Live in the mindset that God knows, wants to, and can supply every need!

Possess the attitude of knowing, and you will own your possessions! God is your Heavenly Father. He is the owner of everything. We are completely dependent on Him, and must, be, therefore, be humble and full of gratitude and thankfulness before Him. Be mindful that all good and perfect gift is from and of Him. You are the head and not the tail, you are above and not beneath. You lend and do not borrow, thus is the believer's status in all things.

Proverbs chapter ten and verse twenty- two says: "the blessings of the Lord brings wealth, and adds no trouble to it." What father among you," says Jesus, "if his son asks for a fish, will give him a snake instead? For everyone who asks receives; he who seeks finds; and to him who knocks, the door will open. "If you who are evil know how to give good gifts to your children, how much more will your Father in heaven give the Holy Spirit to those who ask Him!" Holy Spirit is the best gift of all---desire Him, ask for Him and God who loves to give us good gift will grant our request.

If you have Holy Spirit, you have everything. The ultimate divine source indwells you. You have wisdom at work in you, Omniscience informing you, and Omnipotence enabling you. You have everything you need. If therefore you are counseled by Omniscience; you have all the answers to your life's circumstances. There is no reason to be perturbed. You can simply "be," even as the sparrow "is" or the lilies of the fields--- Be as the sun is "being"--- it never ceases from being the sun. It does not wait for the absence of clouds to shine; it cannot wait! Life goes on---it "is," and to do otherwise will be calamitous.

The eagle as magnificent as it is, it is not without its challenges, but built in is the knowledge to patiently wait for the right wind to soar above unfavorable conditions. You already have all you need to be, so "be!" There is an infinite source of power and wisdom already available to you. You only need to tap into it; be connected to that infinite source.

Jesus said greater things than these shall ye do because I go to my Father. We can command mountains. We can access finances beyond measure. Jesus needed money to pay the taxes. He sent the disciple to catch a fish with the needed currency in its mouth. Divine wisdom would usher you to your provision. Tap in! Rest in the confidence of God the infinite Source. No need to worry about what you should eat, drink or put on.

God knows all things whatsoever you need! The God in you is your reason to hope; you are kept and adequately provided. All your needs He can and will supply---be still, cease from anxiety and worry!

In Psalms forty- six and verse ten He says, "Be still and know that I am God..." We need to find God, and He cannot be found in noise and restlessness. God is the friend of silence. See how nature—trees, flowers, and the grass grows in silence; see the stars, the moon, and the sun, how they move in silence "says Mother Theresa.

Our striving says I do not trust God to be favorable to me. Therefore, I must act on my behalf. I must be independent and do for myself. Stillness is the realization that God is in charge, and in complete control. He knows what is best for me--- He is the one with the perfect plan, and I can trust Him. Do not worry, fret, nor be anxious; our Father is the Lord of Lords, and the King of kings. The earth is the Lord's and its fullness thereof; the earth and all that dwell therein. Believe---every day is pack with miracles, cease from striving, "be still and know that I am God!

"If you limit your choices only to what seems possible or reasonable, you disconnect yourself from what you truly want, and all that is left is a compromise." ~ Robert Fritz

Chapter Nine

Believe consciousness Is the way

There is a way which seems right unto a man, but the end thereof is the way of death. Apparently, this sentence is saying that there is another "way" the right way! Christ has taught us the "way" to live in this world. Being, in the world but not of the world. I have set before you this day, blessing, and cursing; life and death said heavenly Father in Deuteronomy--- choose life! What Father said hundreds of years before, Jesus accurately taught while in this world.

There is the way of the blessing, and there is the way which leads to the curse or death.

Jesus taught in the Beatitudes saying:

Blessed are the poor in spirit for theirs is the kingdom of God.
Blessed are those who mourn for they shall be comforted.
Blessed are the meek for they shall inherit the earth
Blessed are those who hunger and thirst for righteousness, for they will be filled.

> Blessed are the merciful, for they will be shown
>   mercy.
> Blessed are the pure in heart, for they will see God.
> Blessed are the peacemakers, for they will be called
>   children of God.
> Blessed are those who are persecuted because of
>   righteousness, for theirs is the kingdom of
>   heaven. (Matt. 5:3-10 NIV.)

Jesus was saying, all those who possesses these qualities will have supreme happiness and prosperity. They will experience divine favor in this life and in their future life to come. Possess these qualities, and you possess riches untold: Consciousness, Meekness, Authenticity; without guile, forgiving; Peacemaker, Christlikeness; surrendering one's life for a righteous cause.

Now, the opposite of "beatitude" is misery. "Beatitude" means Blessings and Life. Depression is indicative of cursing and death; being afflicted with sufferings. Attesting, that there are indeed dual paths, one to life or the blessing, the other to death or the curse.

Apostle Paul in chapter twelve, and verses two and three asked us not to conform to this world, but be transformed by the renewing of the mind. Why? That we may prove, what is that good, and acceptable; perfect will of God. It is by renewing our minds to the mind of Christ, that we will comprehend what Heavenly Father's perfect will or plan for us is.

His perfect and acceptable will for us is that we love Him with all our hearts. God's loving-kindness is better than life! Thus, by loving Him first, it becomes easy for us to love everyone as we do love ourselves; because we will see the Divine present in all. One John chapter four verse seven to eight, "Beloved let us love one another for love is of God, and every who love is born of God and knows God. He who loves not, knows not God, for God is love. Love, I said before is the most powerful force in the universe. Love heals, shelters the poor, clothe the naked, Feed the poor. It causes wars to cease, it empties prison cells, and it accomplishes the highest good possible.

Love the LORD thy God with all thy heart and thy neighbors as thy self. Considered the law of all laws, for by this all the others are fulfilled. Spiritual, moral and natural laws. All things have been created and arranged for our good. The creator had a perfect plan in mind; It is a beautiful creation and a wonderful life! Seek His kingdom, and you will possess abundant wealth--- Love; Righteousness, Peace, and Joy!

Every individual wants to know what is his or her purpose. For what reason, they came to the earth. It is by renewing the mind, possessing the mind of Christ, that an individual will know God's perfect and acceptable will. I said before, God is love, and therefore, anyone who loves is born of God and knows God. The individual also loves even as Heavenly Father loves. You cannot know God, and not love your neighbor as yourself. It is the perfect love of God which gives us the faith and grace to love others.

Love energizes, it powers and enriches our lives. Like everything else, whatsoever we connect with we become. Throw, an empty bottle into the ocean, soon that bottle becomes filled with it. No electrical appliance will work for you unless it connects to electricity. You may purchase the most expensive car there is, but if there is no battery, without power, it is useless. Subsequently, being in God, you will Love. Thus, having love in your heart; peace and joy will be present also. These three are the commodities of The Kingdom of God.

Love is everything, it is most vital to a whole life, and without it life is meaningless. Love changes everything; where there is war, there will be peace. Love heals the sick, and it shelters the destitute! It forgives, it is not proud. There can be no peace without love, in the absence of it, there can be no joy. Even if you are in possession of all earthly riches, yet, have not loved it is unprofitable. Be in pursuit of God and His love. Seek His peace and pursue it says Psalm thirty-four.

Search for, go after the greatest commodities; love, joy and peace! The kingdom of God is not bread, meat, nor drink; but righteousness peace and joy---which is found only in and through Christ. We are in this world, but not of the world. Let us not be materialistic as the heathen or unbeliever. The old man or egoic self must die. There must be dying to self and the earthly; give up the material for the immaterial. Jesus in John chapter three and verse three says; "you must be born again." That which is born of the flesh is flesh, and that which is born of spirit is also spirit. Inner transformation must take place to be born anew.

There must by necessity be the dying to all things material. A crucifying, then resurrection, and ascension. Yes, this is the path of Christ. Jesus laid down His life, so must each of us--- to enter the realm of pure light. "Whomsoever shall come after me," said he, "let them first deny themselves, and take up their cross" (Luke 9:23.)

Therefore, being surrendered to the renewal

process--- Shedding, old worldly conditioning, and caterings for the ever-evolving spiritual self. We rise into the higher realm. The realm of the Divine---where all things are possible. Each of us coming into spiritual maturity. Ascending into the light of God---growing from glory unto glory, unto glory! The Spirit, Mind, and Body must undergo renewal. The new life is a life of hope and future. The quality of life where there is no limitation--- for nothing is impossible, and the reality is out of this world; far beyond imagination! Life more than abundant, wholeness; nothing missing, and nothing broken. Exceeding, all we can ask or think.

Made into the righteousness of God by Christ. There is a commitment to the transformational process; not conforming anymore to culture, norms nor forms. Continually, the opportunity of the renewal process is available. There is always repentance or the privilege to return. Unfortunately, it appears our changes mostly come through adversities. Typically, by hardships, because many people will not otherwise be heedful.

We have this limited evaluation of life; that things are either right or wrong. I believe that is what fuels our frustration and our negative responses to what we go through.

The idea of right or wrong says that: *One-* if it is deemed bad we will be sad, angry, and frustrated. Consequently, we are being tormented, because of the so-called evil that is happening. Therefore, choosing to resist or retaliate; instead of deciding to go through due process. *Two-* If it is good, the responses will be favorable; I will be glad and happy. Naturally, the individual is being controlled by their circumstances. He or she is not in control. We must learn to meet life's conditions from a higher level.

According to Divine plan, all things are accomplishing a perfect work. Regardless of what we are going through, do not cast Judgement; saying this is bad and that is good. Instead, when faced with our various struggles---let us count them all joy! Advancing, and rising upward; for we are the light of the world. No longer a mere man, therefore, responding not like unbelievers. I said before; everything is working for a favorable outcome, nothing is bad. It is all good, which works for your best interest. It is only a matter of perspective---a matter of believing in the way things are! Accept it as so, and learn to ride out the storms---they won't last always.

Observe God in the fires of your life, and prove if He will not safely usher you through. He has promised, never to leave nor forsake you. He will keep, and bring you through the storms! I speak to you based on my experiences, Scriptural revelations, and the teaching of sages. Hence concluding, that I am in control of my life, and what happens to me, even more so, my response to what am experiencing.

I am a full participant in what is going on in my life and not merely an observer. Also, I have learned that I do not have to war against what is going on. For ultimately all of what is happening is executing the desired purpose. I have learned how to be still; observing the presence of 'I Am That I Am' in all things. Watchfully, tracing my steps--- seeing why, when and how I got to here. As well, paying close attention to the present, and intentionally giving of my best, in "being" my best. My evaluation is that I could not have made it without the helper that is all wise, all powerful and ever present. Thus, I declare, greater is He that is in me than he that is in the world!

There is no bad experience when it is achieving a desirable outcome! Each of what is taking place is unfolding self, true self. In quiet stillness, Observing, knowing, and choosing the "I" I will be in eternity. Yes, beloved, for thus we are eternal beings, spirits having human experiences. Our physical lives and experiences are not all to our lives; we are much more than flesh, and blood. We have come from an unknown but will return to Christ whom we shall know, and we will ourselves be known as He is known!

We all are experiencing the same thing; that which is common to all man. There is nothing new under the sun. Neither you nor I have ever gone through situations or experiences that are entirely new to humanity. What you are going through may be new to you; in that, you have not experienced it before. Others have encountered and are facing the same circumstances. It may be new to you but not to humanity. You will be very surprised to know that someone very close to you is also going through the same thing. This very moment someone in your sphere has a similar situation. What is happening happens to everyone, you are not unique. The only uniqueness here is our response to the situation.

Therefore, knowing that your life consists of more than cause or effect. You are an active participant in what is happening. Take responsibility, be conscious; awaken to who you are. Spirit clothed in earth skin; of limitless power and possibilities. Be predetermined in your heart concerning your success; it is already determined. Thus, only you can prevent your expected outcome. Be present and poised; looking expectantly for your pleasant change. Yes, with trust and confidence in God's ordained plan for your life and all creation; the whole universe is in support of your feat.

You are co-creator with God in this aspect of your life. Thus, it is mostly up to you---you choose! Will, I doubt God and die? How can I, when He is my hope, my ultimate source, my Strength, and my all? For, greater is He that is within me than he that is in the world. My consistent success and prosperity are possible. Nothing is impossible for me if I am in Him and He is in me. In Him, I live and move and have my being, and No- thing can pluck me out of His hands! The same higher power which holds the moon and sun and stars and all the Galaxies in place. The All Intelligent Source which sustains and protects all things--- great or small, preserves you and me. Purposefully we are kept by Him; therefore, all is well---be still and know that "I AM THAT I AM" 'is" and move up to a higher realm in Him.

The Sun does not self-talk saying to itself; "Today I am going to shine my brightest!" No, neither does it worry about the clouds in the sky that might block or obscure its splendor from time to time. It does what it is to "be," without fail. In all fullness, in all its capability, and without reluctance it is brilliant at all opportunity; all the time every day! It shines, it "is"! I call on your "being" to awake: Musician and harp, pen and paper, Kings and Queens, princesses and princes---Lawyers, administrator and clerks; physicians and nurses---wake up! Whatever the instrument or tool, male or female. Destiny is calling your god-self, gifts, and talents. "Be" all you are called to be---"be" you on purpose!

There is that is-ness in all the universe, and this is the "way." An "Is-ness" the way to be surrendered--- to being your true self, and cease from identifying with the material world. You are more than--- greater than things. Things in themselves will not enrich your life. Your being is calling for greater--- come up higher, you are from on high, for higher. Conscious, or Spirit self is the whole and true self. The self that "is" god, perfectly whole, unblemished, all wise and all powerful. "Is it not said that ye are gods?" (Psalm 82:6) You are a child of the universe--- you have a right to be here, and whether or not it is clear to you no doubt the universe is unfolding as it should..." Desiderata.

Pure essence fills you, that glory in the song--- the gap between the cords. The savor in the salt---that brilliance to the light! "Be" that which gives meaning and adds real richness to life---be that, salt of the earth---the illumination of the world.

Something will bring us to our surrender. Not to humble us, no, not that notion. Not being forced, but rather causing us to see, know and comprehend who we are, and who God is. Causing a surrender to who He is, in, to, through, and around us. And who we are to Him, in Him, and of Him; apprehending what He is accomplishing in us. Let me reiterate: We are not forced or coerced, as is commonly taught, not at all. God has given us a free will to choose. He will not violate His laws. Rather it is that heavenly Father lovingly pursues us; revealing Himself to us. Desiring to be united to us.

Deuteronomy chapter thirty: "I have set before you this day, death and life, choose life. God has yes set "the way" for all, would you choose His way? Life is so precious and beautiful; a melody if lived in the "way" Omniscience has ordained for all His creation. Hence our frustrations with life are that we want what we want, our way. Craving and striving after this and that, restless and fearful. Just because, we've chosen our way! We have chosen the path of our will or ego instead of "the Way, the Truth, and the Life." God's perfect way. The way of peace, love, and joy in a world where nothing shall be impossible! Living the way---is life in God.

Jesus had said to the disciples in John Chapter fourteen, "Behold I go to the Father" Phillip asked him, "Lord show us the way to the Father, and we will be satisfied." The great teacher responded with this surprising revelation: "And whither I go ye know, and the way ye know." But, Thomas said unto him, "Lord, we know not whither you go; and how can we know the way?" Jesus said unto him, "I am the way, the truth, and the life...." He continued, "I have been with you all this time, and still, you do not know Me? Anyone who has seen Me has seen the Father. How can you say, "Show us the Father?" God will reveal Himself to those who do not distrust Him. Do you believe Him? "If you see me, you know the Father!"

Most do not see God, for they are not looking for Him in their encounters and experiences. Individuals, primarily the fanatically religious are conditioned to seeing God only from a biblical perspective, and other persons' experiences of Him. Even worst their miss understanding notion of scriptures of who God is. Fostering, such a harsh dogmatic attitude about God, people, and the world. Blinding their eyes from seeing God; they are unable to see Him in other places or other people. Hence adversity is the primary catalyst for most people's conversions. It is in adversities that many of us are driven, pushed or propelled into the highest transformation possible. That of willingly laying down, or crucifying of our material life. Nicodemus had a similar problem---remember? Jesus said to the rich young ruler Nicodemus, "You must be born again!"

There are no shortcuts to entering the realm of the Kingdom of God. The realm of wholeness, where we are becoming like God---perfect even as He is perfect. And Manifesting the superabundance of God on all levels. Exceeding limits and imaginations. Having the laws of God's love working in our hearts and lives. Nicodemus desired the kingdom. He wanted to achieve the realm of life more abundantly, but he seemingly had difficulty leaving the material. Many of us are today bound to the material world, and would not surrender or give it up for the kingdom of God. You cannot serve two masters; you will love one and hate the other.

Behold I have set before you this day life and death, blessings and cursing---choose life says Deuteronomy Thirty. This Scripture gives us proof of the existence of the spiritual and natural laws or principles of God; which is at work in our world and lives. Let me point out that obedience to God or His laws is a must if we would walk in the favor and the superabundance of God's blessings. It is not possible to violate Universal principles and yet have them be favorably at work for us. When we disobey Divine laws, we forfeit our rights of the blessings of love, joy, and peace. The choice is yours to make, choose Life the blessing, or Death the curse. God says, "Choose life!" Heavenly Father, wants you to enjoy His blessings, of life more abundantly.

Heavenly Father has a plan for each of our lives; it is one that is perfect and will not bring us harm---His plan is one of prosperity; hope, peace, and destiny, according to Isaiah twenty-nine verse eleven. That is a life of complete wholeness---nothing broken or missing. The manifest good will and loving kindness of God. His loving-kindness is better than life. So consistently choose His loving kindness over all earthly riches. Be greater than your desire. Desire is a punishment unto the fallen, a tormentor of the soul. Rise above the senses, and you'll have dominion--- you will rule!

In Genesis chapter nineteen God had brought judgment on Sodom and Gomorrah; but saved Lot and his family. They were instructed not to look back. Regardless of what sounds they heard, they were to keep moving forward, and not look back. Lot's wife looked back, and consequently became a pillar of salt. Therefore, fix your attention on what is above, not on what is beneath; here moth and rust corrupt, and thieves break through and steal. The Apostle John instructs that we, "Love not the world or the things of the world." He says in first John chapter two and verse fifteen; that those who love the world does not have the love of God in them.

Consciousness speaks to a non-striving posture. Not clinging to money, and the tangibles of this life. Jesus' command yet remains: "Seek ye first the kingdom of God..." (Matt.6:33.) The kingdom of God is righteousness, peace, and joy in Christ! Thus, the one who is pursuing God and His Kingdom is one that is surrendering to the perfect, acceptable will, and "way of Christ." They are non-striving! Not chasing things, but rather the righteousness of God in Christ. Let us pursue the principles of God that are at work in all things. All that is needful for life and godliness are already awaiting us. It is the rebirth that Christ offers; not the mere saying of "accepting Jesus." It is the "way" of being---being greater than the world. Living in the world but not of the world, this is the biggest miracle of all.

"The Lord is a sun and shield, He gives grace and glory, and no good thing will he withhold from they who walk uprightly." (Ps.84:11.) Believers, the ones following the path of Christ are therefore contented. Whatever state they may find themselves. In little or much, and little is much, and much is more than enough! The couple fishes and loaves were considered sufficient only for a boy's lunch. Notwithstanding, In the hand of, infinite wisdom; receiving it, He offered thanks, distributed, and it became to the multitudes more than enough--- with leftovers.

This inexhaustible source is resident in your life. Significantly, we must live by this knowing. Knowing the way of Christ, the I AM; cast therefore all your cares upon Him for He cares for us. Anchor all your faith in Him! Hebrews Eleven and verse six says; "without faith, it is impossible to please Him, and He who comes unto Him must believe that He "is" and that He rewards those who diligently seek Him.

The kingdom of God operates and functions in dominion authority in all things. It is which "lets" as the Christ the living Word had spoken in his creation, "Let there be light and there was light!" Constantly, and naturally without fail, is this "word" at work in all things. The Sun by day gives light and the Moon by night illumines. Jesus taught "I Am" the way the truth and the life, no man comes to the Father but by me. No man can come but through "I AM" the Living Word, the Christ! This state of being I present to you is life in harmony with God and all things as they are. When one is in harmony with God, they demonstrate love and compassion. Peace is present no matter what may be going on. In the present of otherwise difficult circumstances that person is trusting and therefore is at peace. He or she is not easily distracted or shaken.

There exists a reality, what is happening is not worthy to be compared to what lies ahead; therefore, counting it all joy! What is going on in my life is accomplishing a greater good. Hence, in everything, giving God thanks! If the mind continues to focus on these truths--- fear will not bombard the mind. For it is fixed upon the reality; that, all things are as they should be, and are always working for my best. Intentionally, surrendering each moment to live in The I AM THAT I AM. Heavenly Father, is all the resources you will ever need. Trusting the LORD with all your hearts, and lean not on your understanding. In all your ways acknowledge Him, and He shall direct your paths. (Prov.3:5.)

There are a couple of scriptures verses most of us have learned from our youth. I hope that these will become again fresh in our hearts. One such reference is Psalms Chapter twenty-three, verse one which states: "The LORD is my shepherd, I shall not want;" In other words, I lack nothing. This verse says it all---the Shepherd is adequately capable, and he is well able and willing to care for; provide and to protect. He attends me with loving kindness---I lack nothing! Therefore, I have rest in the worst of life's circumstances.

Psalm chapter one says the individual who does not follow the advice of the wicked or take the path of sinners or join a group of mockers is blissful. Verse two further says, "his delight is in the Lord, and in His law, he meditates day and night. Such persons are as trees planted by the river of rivers that brings forth its fruit in season. The abundant blessing, favor, and loving-kindness of Heavenly Father are daily manifesting in the lives that are exerting in His principles.

Joshua Chapter One and verse eight God told Joshua the secret to success. He said, "This book of the law shall not depart from your mouth, but you shall meditate on it day and night so that you may be careful to do according to all that is written in it; for then you will make your way prosperous, and then you will have success." By practice, I know that consistent success comes from knowing, and being guided by Divine principles.

Jesus in John thirteen and verse seven said, "if you know these things, happy are you if you do them." Practice these laws, adherence to these principles will open your life to more than abundance. There is an open heaven unto those who practices the way of Christ. Indeed, your life becomes more than plentiful; full of love, joy and peace; happiness, contentment, gratitude, and compassion! The riches of the earth will, as a result, fill your life.

The kingdom's path is by way of the cross---surrendered or crucified, repented and committed. Living in nonconformity to the world, possessing a renewed mind; actively, demonstrating it by our living.

I repeat, be mindful to observe God's presence in every aspect of your life. In that way, you will always be full of gratitude. Thus, will goodness and mercy following you all your days. Continually Jesus the Christ was exercised in Divine laws. In all things, He was determined to do the will of His Father who had sent him into the earth. All His works were that of the Father, for the two are but one. Whosoever sees the Son, sees the Father. Committing your ways always unto the Lord He shall bring it to pass for you. Casting all your cares upon Him always; for He cares for you. He is particularly interested in your good outcome.

Always he offers His salvation; delivering, rescuing, providing, protecting and restoring. You are not alone, nor are you forgotten---your Heavenly Father is well acquainted with you and all that concerns you. Never, never will He leave you alone. All things are working for your good (Rom. 8:28.) So be glad in all things; in all conditions and circumstances---nothing will be able to separate you from the love of God which you have in Christ, says Romans chapter eight. It translates to life more abundantly. A life lived in the supernatural realm, where every day the miraculous is experienced----never defeated and always victorious---coming out on top all the time. Every day is presenting inexhaustible possibilities for miracles--- be that miracle! The most fulfilled you will ever be in life is to hear someone say; "you are my miracle--- the answer to my prayer." That tells me that I am walking on my path of destiny; "being" and doing what God has appointed me to "be."

Recently I passed by a homeless man, he called to me, engaging my attention---he asked me to help him with some antibacterial cream. I was willing to purchase the medications for him, even going with him to the pharmacy. However, I was prompted by the Spirit of Christ to do more, and so I did. I was leaving this city in two days. Therefore, I moved urgently to improve the life of this young man. I got out very early in the morning before I would leave and he was there in the place I left him the evening prior. I walked up to him and very carefully awaken him from his morning sleep. He opened his eyes fixing his gaze realizing it was me and that I came as promised. With a very broad grin on his face, he said, "my mother; you are such an angel to me this morning!"

I know he had many disappointments as dreams of healing and rehabilitation were time and again dashed. I gave him the goods I promised and told him to get showered, change his clothes and I will meet him in about an hour. He was excited---- glad as though all was made right. I came back to our spot about an hour and a half later waited for a while and did not see him. Not seeing him, was very disappointing for me; as I 'll be departing the city the next day.

For all that evening, I could not get over the disappointment and grave concern. So, I decided to go into town that night. Surely there he was sitting on the window sill of the restaurant. He recognized the car, and he poised himself, his face lit up, and as I approached him, he said, "my mother, I made several attempts to leave, but I could not move." He was so happy, yet he sobbed as he said, "you are a miracle; thank you!" He was a different person.

There were hope and trust in his eyes again. That is what living the way of Christ is about; love, mercy, and grace---compassion! I hug this young homeless person. I, a once fear-full, arrogant, critical and judgmental person, I am delivered to be a deliverer. The Christ in me is the Christ to you! The Christ in you Is the Christ to him or her; I am compassionate.

The, I AM, the way, the truth, and the life is no respecter of persons. Christ used me to bring a miracle of compassion; love, mercy, peace and grace to a homeless young man. You can be someone's miracle too. Ellis is now on his way to being someone's miracle. Choose to be someone's miracle---don't just wait for a miracle for yourself; plan to be a deliberate change agent for someone! There are opportunities everywhere.

There are many whose greatest blessing is hope. So many are at this moment faced with challenges unknowing how they are going to make it through.

Like the girl who will find love in all the wrong places because she has not seen the right love. The one who is about to take his life because he does not see a way out of his misery. The daughter faced with the challenge of caring for her sick parent, and cannot feed her babies. The homeless on the street desiring medicine, and healing for his gangrene feet. The individual terminally ill, and is living with a death sentence. Who will go, who will "be" servant? In all our challenging times, God gives the necessary graces. It comes to us mostly through others who would allow themselves to be that blessing; to be that miracle.

John writes in the New Testament saying, "Beloved I wish above all that you would prosper and be in health even as your souls prosper." The blessed and prosperous is a life unselfishly lived. We must all ascend to the highest realm, that of non-materialism. Not striving for things, but rather living compassionately; being a tributary of God's love and grace to others. "Let each of you esteem and look upon and be concerned for not [merely] his own interests, but also each for the benefit of others." Says apostle Paul in Philippians chapter two and verse four.

The realm of miracles is that of living from the heart, one of love; compassion, grace, and mercy. Demonstrating the love of Christ in us; we love the Lord with all our heart and our neighbors as ourselves. To share the love of Christ; His "salvation" with others is the greatest miracle possible. His salvation, the way by which He fashions us like Himself. We are all called unto greatness, the greatness of life in

Christ. Being one with Christ; being perfect as our Heavenly Father is perfect.

The spirit or the way of Christ is self-sacrificing; humble and obedient to God. Thus, apostle Paul calls us to complete Christ-likeness, Philippians Chapter two reads thus: If there be therefore any consolation in Christ, if any comfort of love, if any fellowship of the Spirit, if any bowels and mercies, Fulfill ye my joy, that ye be likeminded, having the same love, being of one accord, of one mind. Let nothing be done through strife or vainglory, but in lowliness of mind let each esteem other better than themselves. Look not every man on his own things, but every man also on the things of others.

Let this mind be in you, which was also in Christ Jesus: Who, being in the form of God, thought it not robbery to be equal with God: But made himself of no reputation, and took upon him the form of a servant, and was made in the likeness of men: And being found in fashion as a man, he humbled himself and became obedient unto death, even the death of the cross.

The teachings of Christ echoes through to us today. Like a beacon, it thus beckons to all, "Ye are the light of the world, a city that is on a hill cannot hide. "Therefore, let your light so shine before men that they may see your moral excellence and praiseworthy, noble and good deeds and recognize and honor and praise and glorify your Father Who is in heaven" (Matt. 5:13-16.). Be that light of Christ---you are someone's miracle. "Be" the light that gleams through the darkness!

Chapter Ten

Prayers and Meditation for Beginners

How to Meditate: Ideally create a location where you meet with God daily. Create your unique place; adding music, light, and books such as Bible or other reading materials of spiritual interest. If you do not enjoy sitting in a single position for long; you may choose walking meditations instead, for example, you may walk several times around a small pond or flower bed. Or standing, on the seashores, can be exceptionally awe inspiring.

The key is to be comfortable, and quiet, relax and focus without distraction or interruption. Sit as may be conveniently comfortable for you. Taking deep breaths as you inhale, breath out slowly, put your focus on your breathing; and quiet your thoughts. You will from time to time find your mind may stray and wander, do not become frustrated by that, it happens to all of us; just return to your breathing. Meditation is a skill that you continually train in and develop. Never give up---there are too many benefits.

Understand meditation is not only for the time you sit. But it continues throughout each day. It is the way you live:

Always being mindful; practice your core values, Thus, If you are Christians practice the "way" or principles of Christ. Daoist practice the teachings of the way etc. Being compassionate, grateful, observing God's presence in all things and people. Demonstrate love one to the other; being Kindly affectionate!

Be greater than your adversities. Thus, you are in control. Do not fret, complain nor retaliate. But, be thankful, trials are serving to usher you into your greatness. Observe with patience and diligence, being the greatest expression of Christlikeness.

The Lord's Prayer Meditations:

Taking your favorite position. Get relaxed and comfortable. Focus on your breathing, after you have reached your desired quietness, observing God's presence. Pray the Lord's prayer through the end once. Then you say one stanza at a time; after each sentence of the prayer return to your breathing (about four times, inhale and exhale)

Return to the next sentence of the prayer, return to your breathing (four times inhale, slowly exhale) repeat until you have completed the prayer.

Our Father who is in heaven Hallowed be Thy Name. (Breathing, inhale and exhale four times) Thy kingdom come, (Breathing repeat) Thy will be done on earth as it is in heaven. (breathing, inhale and slowly exhale four times) Give us this day our daily bread (Breathe, inhale, exhale four times) forgive us our debt (Breathe) as we forgive our debtors (Breathe, inhale, exhale four times) For Thine is the Kingdom the Power and the Glory. (Repeat X 3, or as you'd like to)

"I AM THAT, I AM" Meditation:

Take your position, sitting on a chair whatever suits your physicality. Breath as instructed previously.

Firstly, focus on God the Father, love; honor, praise and thank Him." I Am," "That," "I Am". see Him for all that He is, return to "I AM." (repeat)

Secondly, focus on yourself when you say "that" see yourself as perfectly and wonderfully made of God. Picture yourself as you desire, then return to "I am."

Repeat the above as many times as you deem useful.

For example, I am (that) abundant I am! I am (that) happy I am! I am (that) Healed I am! Say it until it changes your emotion, it is key. Believe and respond with joy as though you have it already.

Healing and Energy Activation Meditation:

Posture yourself as instructed above. Sit in your quiet place, be comfortable, still, breathing: inhale and exhale about four times focus on your breath. Move your attention to the Base of your spine or Root energy center. Breath four times into this area as though to breath life into it. Move up to the area just below the Belly Button---breath four times into this area then go to the Solar Plexus, just above belly button, then go to the Heart---breath four times into this amazing organ. Repeat for four times. Go to the area of the Throat, then the area just between the Brows or Third eye, then to the top of the Head or Crown.

There are Seven energy centers in your body. So be sure to identify these energy centers. Allow the energies to flow through the crown center, then moving the energy in reverse down to the base again---breathing, again four times as in the ascent--- Crown to the Brow or Third eye, Throat, Heart, Solar Plexus, to the area Bellow and down to the Base energy center. This meditation will enhance your intuitiveness, mental sharpness, and your dreams will become more heightened. As a matter of fact, you will begin to remember your dreams, growing spiritually alert and insightful. You will move into the higher spiritual realm.

Love- Healing Meditation:

Please follow the basic instructions directly above.

Focus on feeling love---loving every organ as you ascend from the base energy center to the crown. And then reverse the action down to the base or root.

(beginners may practice for ten minutes twice per day, and increase as you desire to twenty minutes, then thirty minutes twice daily.) Meditation is a developing ability or skill. It is not a simple thing; therefore, it requires great determination and discipline patience. With time, you will develop and improve, and it will get much easier. Do not quit, stick with it and unmask your inner strengths and powers, as you ascend to wholeness; in the higher realms of the spirit. The realm where nothing shall be impossible unto you; welcome to the kingdom of heaven! Using the following diagrams visualize your body's organs, their locations, and functions. Also, identify the seven energy centers of the body, this will greatly benefit you, and adding significantly more meaning to your meditation.

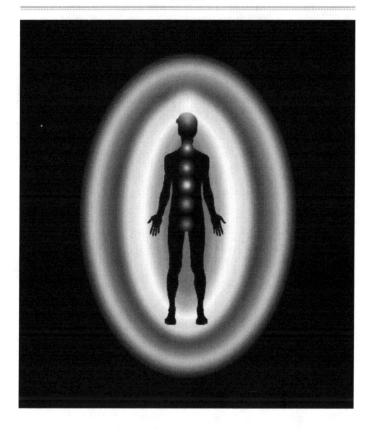

Thus, says the Christ: Whatsoever you will believe when you pray, believe that you have received and it will be so for you. Belief is faith--- acting now. You have whatever you believe in your heart--- now!

Other Books by the author:

Daily Living God's Presence
Daily Living God's Presence Devotional "Courage"
Preparing for the Bride Groom

Printed in the United States
By Bookmasters